The Workplace Family

A Framework for Getting the Best
from Your Employees

The Workplace Family

A Framework for Getting the Best from Your Employees

BY: Tom Collins

ISBN 978-0-557-88508-4

I
ACKNOWLEDGEMENTS

This book would not have been possible with out the generous support and assistance of the following people:

Kendyl Goldston, my administrative assistant for over 18 years who is probably the only person in the world who could sort out my unique approach to grammar, punctuation, and spelling and convert it into text that normal people can understand.

Doug Bennett, my protégé and successor at Scripps Institution of Oceanography who reminded me of components of the environment we had and helped me to describe the lessons herein in the way that he and I had discussed them over the years which made the discussion in the book simpler and more understandable.

Chuck Colgan, creator of Scripps' award winning science publication "Explorations: Global Discoveries for Tomorrows World" and the equally lauded science documentary video series of the same name who contributed his invaluable professional criticism and editorial advice.

Karen Collins, my lovely and infinitely patient wife who generously gave me sufficient release time from my "Honey Do" career to complete the manuscript.

▌▌

DEDICATION

This book is dedicated to the wonderful family we shared in the administration at Scripps Institution of Oceanography. May you always remember, "Once you become a part of the Scripps Family, it is a life sentence."

III

PREFACE

I wrote this book because I had to. It was a compulsion. The reason is that I believe I have created an approach to managing people that not only stimulates them to do their best, but also gives them a good, happy, and self-actualizing work life. Developing and implementing this program within my own organization at Scripps Institution of Oceanography gave me a sense that I had made a contribution in my life that will never leave me, a contribution which goes far beyond the contribution I, and my staff, made to the successful operation of the institution.

LUCKY

This book grew out of a talk I gave during a University of California (UC) system-wide conference on the quality of work life. About 500 managers and human resource professionals from throughout the university attended the conference. I was one of three speakers from the entire UC invited to describe how we had created an extremely positive work environment for our employees. Since then I have been invited to several other professional meetings to give the same talk.

The title I chose for this speech was "LUCKY." There are many reasons why I feel lucky. I have a great wife and family. I spent most of my career working at a great place – Scripps Institution of Oceanography. I knew in my heart that if I did a good job, I was contributing to the success of science that was vitally important to the future of mankind. I have had continuous advancement in my career. I lived in a really great antique craftsman house in one of the best areas of San Diego. I drove really cool sports cars. I have had good health. And much more.

But, all of these are secondary to the fact that I am lucky because as a manager I have had the opportunity to create a new and unique approach to the management of people. I believe this approach has been a major factor in my career being exceptionally successful in a practical sense. But, far and above, the most important part to me is that it gave me the opportunity to achieve that success by making people's lives better. To me this is the ultimate accomplishment. Yes, it was good to be a success in my career, but I might have been successful in many other careers. Maybe I could have been the CEO of a major corporation or been the founder of my own company and made a seven, or eight, or X-figure income. But, frankly, I don't think any of those measures of success compare to the personal satisfaction I have received from giving to people the kind of work environment that makes their lives better. This is really the bottom line for me. It has certainly made my life better, and as I look back, I know I did something really worthwhile with my life. That will stay with me for the rest of my life.

I had to write this book because I felt a profound need to share this approach with other managers so that they too could be LUCKY and give their employees a good work life and experience the same rewards I did. In short, in a small way, I hope this book will make the world a better place for people in their jobs and careers.

For those of you to whom the idea of making it possible for people to be happy in their work lives is appealing, I will state categorically that my approach will help you to do that, and as a secondary benefit, your career will be wildly successful. Simply, as managers we rely on people to do the work of our organizations, and if we can get their best, then we are successful as managers and will be recognized as such. Giving people a good work life is guaranteed to also motivate them to do their best at their jobs. You can do it. Read the rest of this book, and use it as a basis for creating a positive workplace environment for you and your people.

I suggest that those of you who do not find this idea appealing read no further.

With that said, a couple of notes.

First, I created this program in my organization, which consisted of about fifty people. I know for a fact that it works in organizations of double this size and smaller be they for profit, not for profit, government, or voluntary. But, to the best of my knowledge, it has not been tested for considerably larger organizations, although a similar approach is very successful in the Disney theme parks that employ over 50,000 people.

Later in the book I say that I treated everyone, from custodians and groundskeepers to the highest-level analysts and managers in my organization as professionals. This program works if management supports that type of environment. It might not work in an organization where the people are not viewed as professionals. But, as I will argue later, people at the lowest lever of the organization, or at the highest, who are treated as professionals will act like professionals.

I also need to provide a disclaimer. I am not perfect. I am very committed, and I try very hard and for the most part have implemented every aspect of the program I describe. But, I also always see places where I could do better. The ministrations herein may seem idealistic, and they are. They offer an end state toward which we all should strive. I just kept plugging away, and it worked.

Next, I have never heard of nor read about any approach like the one I describe in this book. To the best of my knowledge, my method of motivating people is unique and mine only. If, however, others have come up with and published ideas like this prior to my publishing this book, I apologize and give my assurances that any similarities are purely coincidental.

Tom Collins
Deputy Director, Administrative Affairs
Associate Vice Chancellor, Marine Science
Emeritus
Scripps Institution of Oceanography
University of California, San Diego

IV

INTRODUCTION

I have developed a methodology, call it a strategy, an approach, a program, a gospel – whatever you like – for creating a workplace environment that, if you choose to implement it in your organization, will help you get the best from the people who work for you and at the same time give you a profound sense of personal satisfaction. That environment is a "Workplace Family." The workplace family is defined by a set of positive values. This book is about those values and how "Value Immersion" can make it possible for you to create a workplace family environment in your organization.

YOU CAN MAKE GOOD PEOPLE THE BEST

As managers our career success is based on the performance of the organization(s) we manage – they produce the best product at the lowest cost for example. To accomplish this, the people in our organization must be motivated, committed, hardworking, enjoy their jobs, like where they work and the people they work for and with, and know that what they do is important in the overall scheme of things. In short they must feel that they are part of a larger "family". As managers, it is our job to see that they have these characteristics.

During the early part of my career I became convinced that, while some people come with these qualities built in, many very good people don't, but in fact, the qualities could be created. By immersing people in a comprehensive positive value-based workplace environment these characteristics can and will emerge – they will develop into the kind of worker we want.

I TRIED THEM ALL

I spent most of my career looking for and developing an approach to managing people that has that special motivational effect. The pursuit of my vision started when I was in the MBA program in the Graduate School of Management (now called the Anderson School) at UCLA. I read, attended training sessions, seminars, and professional meetings, absorbing every source I could find about motivational techniques, organizational strategies, psychological and sociological approaches, team-building methods, leadership characteristics, etc. I studied all the latest fads: TQM, One Minute Manager, MBO, Performance Management, est, etc.

Much to my chagrin I was never able to find an approach that really fit the bill, at least not my bill. I watched others' and my own efforts to implement these various programs, only to see them fail in the end. The more I looked at this problem the more I became convinced that there were at least two reasons why they didn't work. Generally, they dealt with one or a few of the characteristics of the total workplace environment that people are exposed to. Also, for the most part, they offered step-by-step prescriptions. So, for example: 1) you make a specific job description, 2) you translate that into an evaluation form, 3) you set down a series of goals/objectives for the employee, 4) during the evaluation you systematically go through and rate the person on the details of that job description and the goals/objectives, 5) then you set new goals/objectives for next year, 6) on, 7) and so on. My own experience has been that these types of prescriptive processes tended to be complicated, burdensome, and ineffective. They just don't work, or they only work marginally and then only in certain circumstances.

EMPHASIZE FAMILY, VALUES, AND THE TOTAL ENVIRONMENT

I found the real answer to the question of how to motivate and get the best from your people through direct observation of the most successful real life organizations. The one characteristic that I found in every one of these was that the members all felt that they were part of a "family". I further found that this family spirit seemed to be a result of a common set of informal values that permeated the work place environment.

Based on these observations I realized and concluded that the best way to motivate members of an organization to give their best is to create a positive value-driven work environment characteristic of a family. Therein a set of well thought out positive values is spread through out the workplace. Immersing employees in this value laden total organizational environment will lead employees to feel that they are part of a larger family. This "Value Immersion" begins with managers internalizing the values themselves and visibly basing their behavior on them. This demonstrates how important the values are and serves as a role model and there by injects, cultivates, and supports their internalization by the whole organizational community. Simply and completely this is the Value Immersion process.

In all of my studies, I have not seen or heard of this method being used. Maybe it has, or maybe it hasn't. All I know is that this concept has turned out to work exceptionally well.

In what follows I will describe the values that I have found to characterize the organizational environment that stimulates the emergence of a sense of family among employees. Notice I said "environment." This concept is key. As I said above, most approaches I have studied do not deal with the total workplace environment they only address a part. Rest assured there are good pieces of each of these, and as I have studied them over the years, the good parts have combined to create a gestalt in my mind, that contributes to my approach. The difference is that I emphasize the values and the total environment rather than the step-by-step prescriptions. "Value Immersion" is simply the process of creating this total environment that is rich in the set of values that define a healthy "Workplace Family"

I hope that you will enjoy reading this book, that it will help you to create a value-driven family environment in your organization, and that it will help you to be successful in your career. But most of all, I hope it will result in a better, more fulfilling life for you and your employees.

CONTENTS

Section One

What You
Want and How
to Get It

*In this section I outline the presumed motivation for reading
this book, what it takes to achieve your goal, and how the
process works.*

CHAPTER 1.1

WHAT DO YOU WANT TO ACHIEVE

As a manager you are very busy; you must have a
purpose in spending the time to read this book.
This chapter outlines the presumptive reasons.

Why are you reading this book? I don't mean to be crass, but let's face it you think it will help get what you want most of all – to be successful in your career as a manager. Why do you want to be successful in your career? Because along with success comes, among other things, recognition, advancement, prestige, and of course, money. As managers, what is success? Bottom line, it is the effective accomplishment of the mission of the organization you manage.

THE MISSION OF ORGANIZATIONS

Whether a for-profit, nonprofit, or a government, the mission of all organizations involves production of a product. You might say, "Yeah sure, if you are in the business of manufacturing widgets, your mission is to put out widgets." Widgets are a tangible product, like cars or washing machines or TVs or …. But, I assert that even organizations that do not produce a *tangible* product still produce a product. You might be producing services, like car repairs, training of some type, counseling, or reports, studies, etc. Each of these services is producing products: fixed cars, trained people, better-adjusted individuals, information for others, etc.

Other organizations, for example, bureaucracies in Washington DC also produce products. While it may appear to many of us that Washington (I will bad-mouth Washington later.) is just a useless sink for money, in fact, Congress produces laws, judges produce rulings, members of the executive branch produce policies or enforcements, etc. And, the staff behind them produces analyses, reports, recommendations, etc. The simple truth is that, if we are gainfully employed in some way, we are engaged in production of a product of some kind. In the simplest sense, the mission of any organization, or subunits of these organizations, is to produce products.

WHAT REALLY MAKES YOU SUCCESSFUL

If you want to be successful in your career as a manager, the organizations you manage must be very good, most desirably the best, at producing a product. And, of course, you want that product to be of the highest quality. It should be the best possible product – flaw and error free. You want to achieve productivity – the greatest volume of output of the highest quality for the least cost, the most and best product per employee, the most efficiently produced, and the best – the *most bang for the buck*. To make this happen, your operation needs to be efficient and flow smoothly. It must be a *well-oiled machine*.

PEOPLE ARE THE PRODUCERS

So, we have established that as a manager, your job is to produce whatever product your organization produces with the highest quality and the greatest efficiency. Well, is there any reader of this book who will deny that the only way to get this done is through people? I have been trying, but am at a loss to think of any activity that doesn't rely on people – maybe an independent blacksmith or a sculptor. But for most of us, we only get our jobs done through people. Even, for example, if you are someone who is responsible for a production line in a car manufacturing plant where robots do most of the work, you still need people to program and maintain the robots. Let's be honest, in order for you to be successful as a manager you have to depend on people around you to actually carry out the day-to-day tasks to *get the job done*. So, your success is really dependent on others. And, your success is dependent on how well you are able to get them to do their jobs as efficiently and effectively as possible. We are talking about motivating people.

The value-based approach to management is the best way I have found to motivate people to do their best. So, please read on.

CHAPTER 1.2

WHAT KIND OF PEOPLE DO THEIR BEST?

This book is about motivating people to do their best.
What characteristics do people who do their best have?
What kind of people can we get to do their best?

In the chapter on what we want to achieve as managers we established that we want to meet the mission of our organization by producing the best product at the least cost. You do this by having people doing their best jobs for you. You need productive and motivated employees. Anything else will result in less than optimal achievement of your success. The question is: how do you get this type of employee?

In the introduction I said that it just comes naturally to some employees, they seem to have been born that way. They give their best no matter what. So you go out and try to hire people like this. Unfortunately, they are in short supply, and the competition is stiff. You are not likely to be able to fill all of your slots with these super-high achievers.

So now what do you do? It is my contention, and I have done it, that employees like that can be created from ordinary people.

WHAT IS THE BEST

"Best" is a general term. There are a whole set of characteristics that you will find in people who are doing their best. What are they?

People who are doing their best want to be doing what they are doing, want to be doing it where they are doing it, want to feel good about their jobs. They are proud of where they are, the organization they are a part of, the product they produce, and the work they do. These people want to come to work, even look forward to it, feel good when they are there, and always strive to work hard and do their best. They are people who are willing to step up and be there when the job needs to be done, go out of their way to meet the organization's needs, put in as much time as needed, and are glad they have done so when they are finished. People in this category have little or no conflict with management or each other and support the organization and its management (i.e., you). They are people who trust in management and their colleagues, are loyal to you and to your organization, and will be long-term employees.

These employees are self-actualizing. They have no fear of management or other employees. They receive both intrinsic and extrinsic reward for doing their best, and they look forward to spending the rest of their lives in your organization. In a word, they are *happy* in their jobs.

Notice, I have said nothing about productivity, efficiency, or product quality. That is because when your workforce has the characteristics described above, they will be doing their best, and these objective/quantitative measures of success come automatically.

WHO CAN BE THE BEST

To be honest, my program won't work on natural-born slackers. You have to have someone you can work with. People who are lazy, want to do as little as possible, just slide by, etc., probably aren't going to respond to anything anyone tries to do.

I can give you an example. At Scripps, the workload in our business offices was substantial. On two different occasions in two different business offices individuals were hired who looked good on paper and did well in their interviews. But, surprisingly enough in both cases, after a week or two, both came to their managers and said: "…you really want me to do all of this?" When the manager said yes, their answer was "Okay, I quit."

So what kind of the people can be transformed? My answer is that you really don't need unique individuals – most people can be transformed into employees who do their best. All we need are people who are not scared away by having to work for a living. Given that, by creating a comprehensive positive value-driven workplace family environment, people will respond. And, I know how to create, and have created, that kind of environment – one that stimulates the development of the characteristics of those who do their best in people who do not fall into the flakey group I described above. I believe that most people are endowed with positive characteristics, but have not been exposed to an environment that fostered their emergence.

YOU CAN MAKE PEOPLE INTO THE BEST

As I write this book I do so with the belief that it is possible to transform ordinary people into people who have these characteristics. I don't think that all who come to you will have them intrinsically. Those who do are few and far between, and if we could hire them all, we would be miraculously lucky. But, most of the time we are not. We have to work with raw material and transform good people into the best. And, we can do it. I have. Just do what is in this book. And, trust me, when you do, your people will be grateful and loyal to you forever, and you will go to your grave feeling that you have done something good with your life.

CHAPTER 1.3

HOW IT WORKS

*People will do their best when their workplace
environment is characterized by a set of positive informal
values that define a family.*

In the past several chapters I have repeatedly said that I know how
to create an environment where you get the best from people and
that this book is about how to do it.

The basic premise is that if one can create a workplace
environment where people feel good about where they work, what
they do, and the people they work with, they will give their best to
the organization. How can such an environment be created?

I have mentioned the answer in passing: Create and immerse
your people in a workplace environment characterized, or defined,
by a set of positive values. Properly defined and implemented, this
set of values will bring people together, give them a sense of
security, instill mutual acceptance and respect for each other,
facilitate their success, give them a reason to want to be at work, let
them know that there is real caring for their well being and much
more -- they feel like part of a larger family. In short this
environment creates happiness for them.

WHAT KIND OF VALUES

Actually, every organization is permeated with values. In
many ways, for example, you could say the formal set of "policies
and procedures" that no doubt occupy a non-negligible amount of
shelf space in your office are a codification of your organization's

values. They are basically the rules that purport to govern people's behavior. These are not the values I am talking about here. What I am talking about are those values that are unwritten, but that really set the tone for how people relate to one another.

The dictionary definition of "values" is:

" . . . ideals, customs, institutions, etc. that arouse an emotional response for or against them in a given society or a given person. My definition as used herein is:

> *"The emotional and behavioral ideals that define the organizations culture."*

> *"The customs of the culture that are manifest in the feelings they stimulate in people about their organization, management, their peers, and themselves."*

> *"That set of commonly accepted behavior expectations that define how managers act toward their employees, how employees act toward their managers, and how employees act toward each other."*

WHY FOCUS ON VALUES

They are that set of ideals that guide manager's decisions as they affect the well being of their employees. They represent the customary way of perceiving situations that occur in an organization. They create a context in which actions by managers or employees are determined and evaluated. They arouse in people an emotional response for or against their organization, management, peers, and/or themselves. The nature of the values in an organization determines whether or not employees care about the success of their organization. In turn, the set of values that exist in an organization affect the morale, productivity, and quality of the output employees' produce.

WHAT ARE INFORMAL VALUES

When I was in graduate school one of the first lessons in my Organization Development (OD) class had to with the *formal organization* and the *informal organization* that exist in essentially all organizations (sorry for the redundancy).

The values codified in the formal policies and procedures are like the formal organization. The formal organization is what you might call the organization chart or, as we called it at Scripps, the wiring diagram. Typically, this is a pyramid-shaped set of boxes starting with the big, big boss at the top followed by the several big bosses that report to him, with each of them having a set of bosses reporting to them who each have several assistant bosses reporting to them who each have a set of supervisors reporting to them, followed by the day-to-day workers below the supervisors. It is what you see in a company's annual report.

But, few organizations actually work like the formal organization chart says they do. For example, I spent essentially my entire career working in the University of California. Each campus had an organization chart with the pyramid-shaped structure, having the chancellor at the top and the faculty at the bottom. However, in reality, one could simply turn that organization chart upside down and it would describe how the university really worked – namely that "the faculty rule," and the chancellor and all of us administrators served at the pleasure of the faculty and did what they wanted – they are the bosses. That is the *informal organization* of the university.

Essentially, all organizations function primarily according to the informal organization. In some cases real leaders, who may not be the big, big boss or one of the big bosses, in reality call the shots. Or despite the pyramid, the organization runs like a democracy, or the organization is really run by the unions, who aren't even shown on the organization chart, or any other permutation you might imagine.

The value system I am talking about is like the informal organization. I call them the informal values of the organization. An informal system of values exists in all organizations. Too often, however, these informal values occur *willy-nilly* evolving with no systematic guidance. As a result they may create a positive work environment where people are motivated to do their best or create a negative environment where people are just *doing their time* and do not give their best or some combination of the two. My whole thesis is based on the observation that these informal values are most important in determining how much your employees are willing to give to you and your organization. It is by deliberately and thoughtfully defining and managing a specific set of informal values that it is possible to create an environment where people not only give their best, but are happy to do so.

WHAT ARE THE POSITIVE VALUES THAT WORK

After years of trial and error, I believe that the set of values presented in this book combine to provide the context where people are motivated to give their best. When they are integrated in a comprehensive way into your organization, they create an environment where people feel good about their jobs, the place they work, the people they work with, and their managers. The idea is to give them a real sense of belonging to a larger family where they know how they fit in and are recognized and accepted for who they are. A sense of pride in the work they do, the work their peers do, and the organization they work for will create feelings of reward and stimulate loyalty. They need to be made to feel safe from retribution for honest mistakes and safe from other employees who might threaten their security. It is important that employees know that management is caring for them and sincerely has their best interests at heart. Management must let people know they support the concept that their people's whole life, work life and home life, is important and cannot be separated. If people are treated with honesty as professionals who are given the freedom to organize and handle their jobs in the best way they can, they will perform as professionals. If people can find pleasure, enjoyment, and fun in their work life, they will want to come to work. And, if they believe that they have a future in your organization, they will want to stay on.

It is clearly not possible to legislate and codify a body of rules that create this kind positive value-based workplace environment that will achieve these goals. It is, however, possible to create and immerse people in a culture characterized by informal positive values. I have observed in my own organizations and other successful organizations that when these elements combine, people will naturally, spontaneously, and happily do their best; and when they do their best, all of the feelings above will be reinforced. It simply requires that the set of informal values in the organization be managed so as to extinguish negative values and maximize those that are positive

So that's how it works: Integrate a set of positive values into your workplace environment that creates a culture where people can self-actualize by being part of a safe, rewarding, and supportive community, and they will give their best.

In the following chapters I will describe the specific values I have identified that, when taken together, make up the informal value system I have found works best to create a sense of family among your employees. Throughout the descriptions of each value, I talk about how that value should be implemented. Then there is a whole chapter in section four that talks about implementation in an overall sense.

Section Two

Values

In this section and Section Three a comprehensive set of values is presented that define the positive value-based workplace, which characterizes the family environment that we wish to create in order to accomplish our goal of getting the best from our employees.

CHAPTER 2.1

WE ARE HONEST

One of the most important components of the positive value -based family we are striving to create is trust. An environment of trust requires honesty.

One of the most important rules that a manager should follow is: "Be honest with your employees." People always want to hear the truth, even if it is bad news. If they catch you BSing them, you are done. They will never trust you, will not give you their all, will not be loyal, and will end up going to a job elsewhere. It should also be expected that your employees be honest with you and each other. Certainly, if you caught one of your people lying to you, it would be bad for his career. Similarly, if he lies to his peers, they will not respect or trust him. And, the family sprit could not be sustained.

Below I discuss honesty in the context of several examples: giving feedback on performance to employees, making commitments or promises, requiring feedback from employees to the boss. In fact those are just a few of the circumstances where honesty is the best policy. The point of this chapter, however, is that being as honest as possible in any and all circumstances is the best policy and is essential to create feelings of family within your group.

EXCEPT FOR

There is one caveat, and it may be obvious to you. Jim Carey was star of a movie called *"Liar, Liar"* where he had to be absolutely, 100 percent truthful about everything. If you saw the movie, you will recall that it didn't really work out very well for him. His blunt and brutal absolute honesty in relaying his real thoughts were not always the kind we would normally tell people. This is not the kind of honesty I am talking about. We do have to temper our emphasis on honesty with reasonable civility, courtesy, and sensitivity.

SPIN VS. LYING

An important related question is: Is "spin" lying? This has always been a difficult question for me. Basically, the general definition (at least the one used by politicians) is that spin is really not lying; it is trying to put out the best (or worst) possible interpretation of the facts of a given situation. I mention it here because I am not above spinning things. But there is good spin and bad spin. If, for example, a situation is spun so that the truth is twisted so far it is for all intents and purposes lost, it is bad spin and can be as damaging as telling an out right lie. Then there is good spin that, while not doing serious violence to the truth, can help people in difficult situations. In the context of the discussion below, I will show how this works.

BE HONEST IN GIVING FEEDBACK ON PERFORMANCE

Being honest is sometimes the easiest, and sometimes the most difficult, thing we can do as a manager. Easiest is when an employee has done something very well. It is important to be honest in giving praise for his success. That may sound obvious, but I think you would be very surprised at how many managers just don't give this kind of feedback at all or do so only grudgingly.

BAD JOB

On the other side, often managers will give praise or be less than honest in cases of poor performance (bad spin). They do this under the misguided belief that the praise will motivate the employee. Unfortunately, it simply reinforces poor performance and sets low standards. It is essential that managers are up front and frank (i.e., be honest) when overall poor performance or disciplinary matters must be addressed. It is ineffective to "pull punches" or soften the message (bad spin). The employee is likely to miss the point, and thus, have no basis on which to seek improvement.

Regrettably, I learned this the hard way. At one point during my early years as a manager I had a business manager reporting to me who was not doing a very good job of keeping on top of our finances. On several occasions during meetings I mentioned my concern about this to her, but at the same time I tried to complement her in other areas (bad spin). This way, the discussions were a lot easier for me because at that stage in my career I had not gotten used to coming down hard on people when there was a real problem. Instead of focusing on the problem and trying to work together to take corrective action, I chickened out. As you might guess, she didn't get it. Finally, I sat down with the books and much to my horror found we were over $600,000 in deficit. So, I called her into my office and said: "Jamie (names have been changed to protect the guilty and the innocent), I have talked to you three times about my concern that you were not on top of our finances. Now we are deeply in deficit. I am afraid I have to relieve you of your responsibilities in this area, and I will give you one chance to get away clean (in other words, resign or be fired)." She was sincerely shocked, saying: " . . . Gee, I didn't realize you were that concerned." In the end, she chose to resign. You can see that if I would have been honest from the start, things may not have gotten this bad.

GOOD JOB BUT SOME PROBLEMS

What if the job done was good, but not perfect? Do we give praise for the good part and ignore the less than perfect part? Do we focus on the less than perfect part and ignore the good part. Or, do we deal with both to the extent that they contributed to the overall end product – an effective and motivated employee. Here again you might say that the answer is obvious. But, many times I have seen managers' only focus on the good part of an employee's performance. This is more or less what I did in the example above. Although this is not outright lying, it is lying by omission (bad spin). It is sometimes justified as positive spin, but it is not. The outcome is the same – poor performance is reinforced and a lower standard is established. As above, it does not give employees any feedback that they can use to improve.

I have also witnessed many situations in which managers only focus on poor performance and ignore the good part. This approach is often found in environments that are characterized by the authoritarian motivational model such as in the military. By far, it is one of the worst mistakes a manager can make because the employee will feel picked on, belittled, and not recognized or appreciated for the good work he is doing. This lowers morale and affects overall performance in a negative way: "Why should I try harder? The boss only sees the bad part anyway."

That's why dealing with both is the best policy. Employees can use the positive feedback to reinforce their good performance and the critical feedback to make a course correction in order to improve. However, the critical feedback must be provided in a sensitive and supportive way. For example, you might say: "Jimmy, you did a great job of following through with this purchase order, thanks, oh, and next time you might want to double check the spelling, that will make it an even better job." I call this positive spin. You gave the praise and the criticism, not as an explicit complaint about Jimmy's spelling, but as a positive suggestion to double check it next time. The employee will feel good about the praise and, I assure you, will happily double check the spelling because he will want to be praised even more. And more importantly, he knows that the praise will be forthcoming if he does a better job.

The principles here are easy: Don't beat around the bush when there are problems/issues regarding the employee's performance that are truly serious as in the example above. Address them honestly and completely. When good employees show mixed performance, recognize their achievements and point out their weaknesses in a way as positive, non-threatening, and constructive as possible (positive spin). In following these principles you are creating an environment where your employees trust that they will be recognized for their good work and given non-pejorative feedback to improve in problem areas. In this environment people feel comfortable and safe and are anxious to keep getting better and better.

DON'T MAKE PROMISES YOU CAN'T KEEP

Another very important area where honesty is fundamental is in making commitments to people. I have committed errors in this more times than I would like to admit. Often, as managers we want to give our employees a belief that we can do things that we really can't. This is the situation where you might feel uncomfortable saying no, so you cop out by saying you will follow up later, and you never do. Although at the time you may be sincere, in fact, unless you really think you will or can follow through, a failure to do so will give people the impression that you are lying to them. If you really believe you can follow through, and you try hard and fail, you can easily save the situation by immediately going back to the employee(s) and being as honest as you can explain to them how hard you tried, and how sorry you are that you failed. If you just didn't get to it, be honest about that too. They will accept your honesty, and generally forgive you.

As an example, once there was a very distinguished professor who had asked that I get back to him about a certain matter. I didn't for a couple of weeks and eventually, out of guilt, went to his office. He was clearly not too happy with me. I said I was sorry, but I had been trying to get back to him. He said "Oh?" I said "Oh no, I haven't actually picked up the phone. I have it on my list and say to myself: I have to call today. But it just doesn't seem to get done." He laughed and said he knew just how it was; he had the same problem. Here the truth was really the only way to get past his unhappiness with my not getting back to him.

The consequences of failing to honestly admit your mistakes are serious. As I mentioned above, people will loose their trust in you. This makes for a very uncomfortable working environment. While you may be the most strait-up guy around in all other aspects of your management, we all know that bad news travels much faster, with less impedance, and leaves a more lasting impression than good news. The mistrust will be generalized and people will be uncertain and paranoid. This is not the family way and leads to inefficiency, lower productivity, and low morale.

DON'T COVER UP YOUR MISTAKES

There is a tendency in most people to have a hard time admitting their mistakes. Often, people even have a hard time admitting to themselves that they have screwed up, much less to others. But not doing so can be a worse mistake. I have seen people literally destroy their careers because they lied about something they did wrong. Typically, the thing they did wrong was not that serious, but the act of lying about it is what cost them. And, trust me, you will get caught in a lie. As "Honest Abe" Lincoln said, "No man has a good enough memory to be a successful liar." Oh how true that is.

In the world I worked in this was particularly important. If you got caught lying to a faculty member, you were *dead meat*. But, if you were straight up with them, they would almost always accept and respect you for doing so. The professor I mentioned above is one example. Another has to do with one of our most distinguished faculty members who also turned out to be one of my favorite people of all time. He was most friendly and welcoming to me. Even before I officially started at Scripps Institution, he invited me to his home and took me to sea the next day on a one-day cruise for new graduate students. Shortly after I did officially start, he asked me a technical administrative question. I answered, but it was the wrong answer. I later realized it was wrong and immediately went to him with an apology and the correct answer. Well, you guessed it. Soon thereafter he asked me another technical administrative question, and I gave the wrong answer again. Realizing my mistake, I went back to him with another apology and the correct answer. I also smiled and said, "That's two . . . " He looked at me sternly and said, "I know." He then laughed, and so did I. Since then we have laughed about this situation many times, but imagine what would have happened if I had tried to cover up my mistakes. His trust and respect for me would have been in the toilet.

I used professors in these examples, but the same lesson applies to staff below you. If you are not straight with them, it will create a non-trusting environment, which seriously affects people's motivation.

BE HONEST IN COMMUNICATION

It is important when communicating information to employees to be honest even if it is bad news. The important thing is not to exaggerate or minimize the circumstance you are reporting to them.

The easiest example to understand is if your organization is running into difficult budgetary times. Assume that the latest projection suggests a 20 percent reduction in revenue. The first response is to say nothing. This is based on the theory that "ignorance is bliss." Of course, your people will know something is up anyway. And, the rumor mill can make anything look worse. Not saying anything is lying by omission and will have the same consequences as an outright lie.

It is tempting to minimize the truth by saying something like: "Oh yeah, there is a bit of a budget problem, but it won't affect us." You might argue that you are just trying to put a positive spin on the situation, but it is pretty hard to argue that this is a true statement (bad spin). A 20 percent budget cut is serious. Here again, people will ultimately find out you are being less than truthful, and the spin will turn out to have a negative impact.

On the other hand, some managers put the opposite spin on the situation and exaggerate its seriousness. The idea here is to scare the hell out of people so they will work harder to increase revenue or decreases costs. Then when the situation turns out not to be as bad, they will think you are a hero. This tactic will also backfire. First, as I said, people will hear from other sources that things may not be as bad as you say so they begin to lose confidence in you. Exaggerating also causes significant emotional strain in people. That may actually cause them to be less productive because they spend a lot of time worrying unnecessarily when they could be working. Finally, and I have seen this happen, while people will be relieved that things weren't so bad after all, many will be angry:

"Why did you get us all upset when things weren't really that bad?" There goes their trust in you, their loyalty, and their willingness to go all out for you.

So, the answer is "give it to them straight," don't have a hidden agenda, and don't try to con people. It will backfire every time. Tell them the exact figure you are working with. Make sure the level of uncertainty in the projections is clear. Do your best to outline the impact. Assure them as sincerely as possible that you will do your absolute best to protect them (and mean it, and do it). Get them involved in seeking solutions or strategies to minimize the impact. Be as visible as possible in your efforts to mitigate the negative outcomes. And, keep them regularly posted as the situation unfolds. In short, show them that you are being as honest as you can and that you are on their side. I assure you that this honest approach will insure that even if things turn out badly – layoffs for example – morale won't be as damaged as it otherwise would, people will still trust you, and they will continue to give you their best – especially if you treat the affected people humanely.

MAKE IT SAFE TO BE HONEST WITH THE BOSS ABOUT THE BOSS

Positive outcomes are achieved when employees feel they can be honest with the boss. They need to know and believe that they can come to their manager, say what needs to be said, and there will be no retaliation or other negative consequence.

For some managers this is difficult. They are caught up in *being the boss* and are afraid that people will lose respect for them if they show weakness by letting their subordinates criticize them. Basically they are insecure, which in and of itself is a fatal trait for a manager's long-term success.

Also, would you believe that many managers appear to think they are infallible? They think they know it all, but in fact they do not. As I discuss in other chapters, even employees at the lowest level often know more and have better answers than the boss. Those people must feel that they can speak up. As managers, it is of vital importance that we <u>do</u> <u>not</u> surround ourselves with "yes-men" or people who are too scared of us to speak up. This is one of the worst things you can do, and I guarantee that if you do, you will screw up a lot more than if you welcomed your subordinate's feedback. Just like when you give your employees criticism so they can improve, you need honest criticism so that you can improve.

I have always admitted my fallibility and it has worked. I once had a man working for me who came from a military background. In fact, he was a really interesting person. He flew fighter jets and B-52s while a colonel in the Air Force. He was one of the best employees I ever had. When he first came to work for me, he had a little plaque on his desk. On the side facing out it said: "The Boss Is Always Right." On the side facing him it said: "When The Boss Is Wrong, See The Other Side." It was cute and kind of funny, but I made him put it in a drawer in his desk. I said: "Duke (that was his name, kind of cool for a macho fighter pilot!), I need you to tell me if you think I am screwing up. I often go off in the wrong direction, have bad ideas, and want to do stupid things. If someone doesn't tell me, then things get screwed up and I have to waste time solving problems. I will not always follow your advice, but I will always listen. And, no matter how stupid you say I am being, you will never, ever have to worry about my wrath." It took him a while to get used to this, but trust me; he saved my butt many times.

Surprisingly enough (or maybe it isn't surprising) it is not easy to get employees to tell the boss what they think, good or bad. Generally, this is a result of their having been in jobs where their managers would not tolerate people being honest with them. They just weren't used to it. Duke, for example, came from a long career in the military where you just don't question your superiors.

Sometimes more drastic measures are needed. I had one person whose official job description required her to (I am paraphrasing) "...bitch at me whenever you don't agree with what I am thinking, saying, or doing." We had an understanding that she did not expect me to, and would not be hurt if I didn't, take her advice – the buck stops with me – but she should never be afraid to give it. Believe me, she took this part of her job description seriously and always got a "superior" rating during annual review. But, again, as in the case of Duke, she saved my butt many times, and to be honest there were times when I didn't take her advice and later wished I had.

These examples, while true, are a bit extreme. You don't have to put this level of relationship in everyone's job description. But, you can create an environment wherein people realize that being honest and giving the boss feedback is encouraged. In fact, just seeing that the employee mentioned above did not suffer retribution for telling me like it is, helped others to get comfortable with it as well. It takes time.

AN ENVIRONMENT OF HONESTY IS BEST FOR EVERYONE

If you set a good example of being honest, it will most often result in the people below you adopting the same values. In a real sense you create an *environment of honesty* where people are honest with each other (within the bounds of courtesy) and most importantly with you. When people are honest with each other, there is much more mutual respect and mutual support of each other than occurs in workplaces that do not have this characteristic. Sometimes there may be complaints or criticisms of each other. This may lead to conflict, but I have found in every case, if common courtesies are respected, these conflicts are easy to resolve.

Are these not characteristics of a family? Those of you who have raised more than one child know that brothers and sisters (or brothers and brothers or sisters and sisters) do have a way of being honest about their feelings for one another, and as a result conflicts do occur. If the family environment is not seriously pathological, these conflicts are quickly resolved and the siblings love each other forever. In a good workplace environment, the same thing happens. In the end, resolutions are found, and the people end up respecting each other and working together happily.

The more cynical among you will no doubt say: "This is too idealistic and not realistic." To them I say, "It really works." If there is an environment of honesty, if the boss rewards honesty and focuses on resolving conflicts rather than threatening people when they are criticized, people will get along. The reason is that there really is a feeling of safety when people trust each other and believe others will always be straight with them. On the contrary, when there is not an environment of honesty, people tend to mistrust their peers, rely on the pervasiveness of the rumor mill, never feel comfortable about what the other guy is thinking or plotting, etc. In this environment morale is low, people waste a lot of time worrying, and generally are either not motivated to, or cannot, give their best.

The bottom line is that creating an environment of honesty starts with you. If you not only live it, but also talk it up and sell it, you will have created an environment where people feel safe and trusting, believing that they are part of a larger family where "we are all in this together, and we are all trying to be, and help each other to be, the best."

CHAPTER 2.2

WE FIT IN

To foster a sense of family it is important that people know they we fit in -- how their jobs relate to others and their role in the overall scheme of things, not a detailed job description.

One of the biggest fallacies that I see is the belief in managers' minds that if a formal job description is detailed and comprehensive enough, employees will be satisfied and know what they are supposed to do in their jobs. I have always been frustrated with the job description process. This book is about how to manage professionals. I treat everyone who works for me as a professional, and professionals really don't need to be told every detail of their job. In fact, they often resent it when someone tries to do this. It is a form of micromanagement. Professionals need to be given latitude and independence. Yet over time, it appears to me that job descriptions are getting longer and longer with page after page of details. They are proscriptive; specifying in great detail every task the employee is to do. This is such a horrible waste of time. The simple truth is that even with these tomes for job descriptions, most employees still find that they do not describe what their jobs really involve and how they fit in. You do not need a job description to be a part of a family. While I realize that in bureaucracies job descriptions are required, if as a manager you stop there you will be heading up a bureaucracy not a family.

LENGTHY JOB DESCRIPTIONS DON'T WORK

There are many reasons why lengthy job descriptions don't work. First and foremost, it is simply impossible to identify and list all of the day-to-day things that people do in a complex organization. Further, even if you could list everything, in no time, changes in the organization's needs occur and new duties or responsibilities are assigned that were not previously on the job description. Also, it is simply impossible for people, both supervisors and the employees, to remember all of the details in these huge documents. Job descriptions like this generally amount to a simple listing of tasks. They lose meaning, rather than telling how the person fits in. They do not give employees a broader vision of their role in the organization.

As an example, when I first began my career at Scripps Institution of Oceanography (SIO) I was given a six or seven page document specifying in great detail every thing that reported to me, a detailed list of the tasks I could undertake, and a bunch of financial information on how much money was under my control. I read this job description once during my entire 23 years at SIO. It just didn't capture the spirit of what my role in the institution really amounted to and how it related to the overall and the detailed operation of Scripps. In addition, my job evolved over time with new units reporting to me, others moving to other people, general span of control, etc. My official job description was never updated to reflect these changes. Despite this I never once had a hard time figuring out what I was supposed to do, and my supervisors never had to refer to my job description to evaluate my job performance.

WHY ALL THIS PAPER

One of the reasons that human resources people in bureaucracies seem to be requiring more and more details in job descriptions is to protect against grievances, law suits, etc. If, as I said above, it is impossible to list everything that a person does during the day, and that jobs change regularly, then it is also impossible to insure that these kinds of grievances will not happen no matter how many pages in the job description. This belief is really a trap. If the policy is that an employee's job description must completely specify the details of his job, then there are even stronger grounds for grievances. The reality is that the organization evolves over time and changes occur in the day-to-day work of the employee and his job description is not updated, then he is in fact not doing exactly what the job description says. So if he is criticized during an evaluation for some task that is not on his job description he can argue, "that's not my job," and his argument would be sustained. Thus, because successful organizations are dynamic and changing all the time, to achieve the protection the HR people want, we as managers and supervisors would have to spend most of our time revising job descriptions. It is much safer to have a policy that job descriptions are broad statements that allow for flexibility.

WHAT WORKS

The best job description I have ever heard was when President Roosevelt called General Dwight Eisenhower into the oval office, sat him down and said: Ike, I want you to proceed to London, assume command of the allied forces in Europe, and win the war against Germany. Now that's a job description!

Obviously, this example is a bit of an exaggeration. I am not trying to say that we do not need job descriptions. What I am saying is that they should outline in broader terms what is expected of employees, rather than specifying how they should go about their work day. The manager is responsible for making sure employees know what their jobs are, despite job descriptions.

FORMAL VS. INFORMAL

A tautology of management is that there is a formal organization and an informal, or real, organization (remember formal and informal values). The highly detailed job description is like the formal organization. What we need to achieve is an understanding in the employee of what he is expected to accomplish and how he fits into the real organization. By this I mean that we should endeavor to focus on the result of the employee's efforts, rather than trying to specify what the efforts are.

As an example, I had a person reporting to me who was responsible for the underwater diving program at Scripps. In accordance with policy, he had a job description that ran to several pages with details like: check the regulators weekly, rebuild them yearly, inspect the BCs regularly, require at least 12 dives per year to maintain certification, make sure the tanks are certified, and on and on. But, I made it clear to him what his real job was: "I don't care if you work one hour a week or 100 hours a week, your job is to make our diving program the safest in the country. No serious accidents, and definitely no fatalities." I did not have to tell him how to do it. He knew what he was doing or I would not have hired him. And, guess what, we never had a serious diving accident since the program started in the early 1950s, although I didn't expect him to take me up on the one hour per week (just kidding). My point is that you give professionals a job to do, and let them do it. They know what to do. Relying on a job description for the details is a waste of time.

HOW THEY FIT IN

Beyond the formal written job description, it is incumbent on managers to spend time discussing with employees how they fit into the organization – how their jobs relate to all of the others in the group. They need to know where there is overlap, where their work affects others' work, where others' work affects them, and how they can help each other to be successful. After all, what we are really striving for is that each and every one of our people to be successful. They simply cannot do that with a stack of paper as guidance, no matter how detailed. I argue that the more detailed the less effective the job description is. People need a broader perspective; they need to understand in a fundamental way their role and its importance to the overall mission of the organization.

As time goes on, the organization and its mission will evolve. Employees need to know how that evolution affects them. If every time something changes we have to go through and update everyone's job descriptions that is all we would be doing. The ongoing job of a manager is to use personal contact to help people continue to be aware of how they fit into the organization given changes that inevitably occur.

WHAT THEIR JOB MEANS

Beyond helping people to see their role in the overall organization, it is even more important that they appreciate the meaning of their role in the general scheme of things. They need to be able to see the importance of what they do as it affects and contributes to the successful fulfillment of the organization's mission. With the typical bureaucratic job description that understanding cannot be, and never is, communicated. We have to help people to see how important they are. This helps to put more meaning and self-fulfillment into their lives.

Getting back to my diving officer. Although not specifically in his formal job description, it was clear to him that he played a central role in the mission of Scripps. Research diving is essential in oceanography, especially in the biological sciences. He fit into the research and teaching programs by providing essential training, oversight, and management of the diving program. His support made it possible for others to safely undertake the work that they needed to do.

This is one of the most important values needed in creating an environment where people give their best. Think of it – if you just see your job as a series of tasks outlined on a formal job description, then you will simply undertake to carry out those tasks. If on the other hand, you see your job as being important to the overall success of yourself, your peers and colleagues, and the dynamic organization of which you are a part, you will be very much more motivated to do your best. If instead of a detailed proscriptive job description, you are given an overall concept of your mission, how it fits, and how your contribution affects the outcome of all that your group is trying to accomplish, you will be motivated and able to use your intelligence, creativity, and initiative to execute your job in the best way that you can and give the best that you can. This environment gives people a sense of accomplishment, meaning in their work, and feelings of fulfillment. It makes them feel important, useful, and needed – that they are an important part of a larger family. Because this organizational value is that you and what you do is more important than a job description, it provides a key component in motivating people to do their best.

CHAPTER 2.3

FREE TO BE ME

Every member of a family is a unique and special person
who is appreciated for what he brings to the family unit. We
value people for their individuality, respect their ability to
do things in their own way, and encourage them to do so.

I think I can safely say that everyone has their own way of doing things. In fact, I also feel safe in saying that just about all tasks can be successfully completed in different ways.

These observations are key elements of the kind of working environment we wish to create. Allowing professionals to go about their work in their own way is exceedingly important. Both managers and peers within organizations often do not understand the importance of applying these concepts in their day-to-day interaction with employees.

MY WAY IS THE BEST

Managers often have been promoted from lower-level jobs within their organization or did similar lower-level work in other organizations. Thus, during the course of their career they developed their own ways to accomplish various tasks. Generally, they will believe that after years of experience, their way of carrying out a task is the best way. Thus, on seeing another person approach the task in a different way, they have a compulsion, which is difficult to resist, to try and make their subordinate approach the task in the same way they did.

The best example I can think of to clearly illustrate this doesn't come from my work life, but from my home life. My wife and

I both get paid on the first of each month. So, I arranged it so that nearly all of our bills can be paid on the first of the month. Thus there are quite a number of bills (ugh!) to be paid at one time. I am almost always the bill payer and have developed a procedure I use that to me is unquestionably the best. I first open all of the bills, remove them from their envelope, and organize them by categories that map into our family budget spreadsheet: mortgages, car payments, gas, utilities, credit cards, etc. Next, I write checks. We have a checkbook with three checks per page. I write the checks, do not detach them, but leave the three bills between each page with the top one corresponding to the third check on the page. Then I go on to the next page. When I have written all the checks, I go backward through the check book, tear out each check, place an *X* along with the amount paid and the date on the part of the bill to be retained, remove that part of the bill that is to be sent in, mate the check with the bill, and place them in the envelope, lick, and seal it. Once all of the enveloping is done, I go through the pile once and use an ink stamp to put our return address on the envelope, then a second time to place the postage stamps.

As anyone with the remotest sense of organization can no doubt see, this is the perfect process. It is efficient, because it minimizes mixing of steps so, for example I don't have to put the pen down after writing each check; it allows for automatic checking of errors; it makes the process simple and to a large extent mindless; and so on. It is impossible for me to see why anyone wouldn't or couldn't do it this way. Maybe I should be writing a book on how to go about paying the household bills rather than about managing people.

From time to time, when for some reason I couldn't, my wife would do the monthly bill paying. You won't believe how she goes about it. It drives me crazy. She uses the following procedure: randomly takes one envelope from the stack of bills, opens it, picks up the pen, writes the check, puts the pen down, picks up the bill, tears it apart, sets the bill down, tears off the check, picks up the bill, puts the check and bill into its envelope, seals the envelope, puts the bill down, picks up the sheet of stick on return address labels, removes one, places it on the envelope, puts the return address labels down, picks up a sheet of postage stamps, separates one stamp from other stamps, places it on the envelope, then repeats the cycle for the next bill. Honestly, this is about the dumbest way to pay the bills that I have ever seen. Talk about inefficient! I have tried and tried to teach her the correct (my) way, and she either wouldn't or couldn't do it that way. I even ordered her to change. (Ha, ha . . . as if I have the power to order my wife to do anything.)

Well, those of you who are married can imagine how far that got. In fact, what really happened was that she first felt inadequate because she couldn't do it the right (my) way. That made her mad, then she slammed down the checkbook, told me to put it in a place that would be anatomically difficult to accommodate it, declared that if I didn't like it the way she did it, I could do it myself, and stormed out of the room. Thankfully, we didn't get a divorce over this; in fact we made up right away and were able to laugh about it, although she probably won't be too happy that I am using this example in my book. I hope she will understand that I only used it to illustrate my point.

YOUR WAY IS AS GOOD AS MINE, AND DEFINITELY BETTER FOR YOU

The truth is that my wife's way of doing the bills is just as good as mine. In fact, the bills get done, there are no mistakes, it probably takes her no longer than it does me, it is less complicated than my method, and she is comfortable doing it that way. But, my insisting that she do it my way caused her distress and ultimately made her so mad that she just gave up and resigned her position as pinch bill payer.

If you are a manager who insists that employees execute tasks in your way, you are making a fundamental mistake. You are basically saying, "Not only do it, but do it my way or the highway." Employees are no different than my wife. If you try to force them to do things in a certain way it might not be the best way for them. They might try and fail because they just don't see the task in the same way as you do. They would certainly be frustrated because they are no different than you – they think their way is the best.

They are likely to be angry because you reject their suggestions to do it a different way. They are most likely to be demoralized which, of course, affects their motivation and extinguishes the other characteristics of the kind of employee that we want and have described in other chapters of this book. So, while you as a manager might be thinking that if the task was done in your way a greater efficiency could be achieved, the opposite is likely to occur. Productivity will be negatively influenced.

It is vitally important that you let people be who they are. How they do things is a big part of who they are. If you denied them the freedom to be themselves and do things their way, you have created an environment that does not foster, but in fact inhibits, productivity -- the happy, self-actualizing employee that we want is not happy or self-actualizing. And, by establishing the freedom for people to accomplish their tasks in their own way as a central value of the workplace environment, all other staff will treat their peers in the same way, which minimizes conflict and other social maladies.

CHAPTER 2.4

HUMAN AND HUMANE

It is essential to get the best from people, we accept that we are all human, and humane treatment is a fundamental value of our organization.

Have you ever heard people talk about their bosses who seem to believe that there is no life outside the job, who are completely intolerant of mistakes, and who are heartless in the way they deal with their subordinates? This treatment is the antithesis of the family way and obviously, these employees are not happy in their jobs. Do you think they are giving their best? I don't!

Managers who operate like this probably think that they have to be that way in order to get the most work done. After all, if people are always interrupting their work to deal with something in their private life, are having a bad day, or are having trouble concentrating, they aren't totally engaged in their assigned tasks. Mistakes cost money and lost time. If a person is trained to do a job, they should do it flawlessly. And, why not be tough? If people fear the consequences of being on the wrong side of the boss, they will work harder to get their jobs done. This reasoning is profoundly fallacious.

ONLY FOR BOSSES WHO ARE PERFECT

These managers are so very misguided. I sometimes wonder how people like this can be so blind to the simple fact that we are all human. To me this means we aren't always perfect. We make mistakes, are distracted sometimes, have trouble focusing, worry about things going on in our outside lives, have a bad day once in a while, get sick from time to time, maybe get seriously sick, and so on.

Jesus said: "He that is without sin . . . first cast a stone." I would really like to meet the manager who is both intolerant of humanness in others and is completely free of those characteristics. The obvious truth is that there is no such person. But, there are many managers who seem to think they are or at least they act as if they are. They are misguided, because while they are intolerant of the humanness of others, it is in fact impossible for them not to have human characteristics themselves. After all, they are human. In fact, one of the most fundamental mistakes a manager can make is being intolerant of others human faults.

There are consequences of letting your ego get in the way of being a humane boss. The worst consequence of thinking you're perfect, or acting like you think you are, is that everyone knows that you aren't. They will think you're a fool or, more than likely, a particular part of the human anatomy. But, at a minimum, their respect, loyalty, and willingness to work hard for you go right down the drain.

THE INHUMANE BOSS

I have closely watched two leaders who were really *heartless* in the way they dealt with their subordinates. What a truly sad set of circumstances it is that individuals in major executive positions beat up the people around them. One boss berated people in meetings, using cruel and demeaning language when expressing displeasure with their actions, broadly showing disrespect for people, eliminating the jobs of individuals with decades of exemplary service with no sensitivity, even speaking down to them in the face of broad-based support for the individual from people throughout the organization, and much more. In the organizations he led, morale plummeted, and employees were scared to death of incurring his wrath. So much so that they did everything they could to function out of his sight – to hide out and be as invisible as possible.

This means they don't do anything very good, or very bad; they just existed. Were these people giving their best? Hardly.

Other than a pathologically overgrown ego, or a Napoleon complex, I frankly don't know, nor can I begin to explain, why some managers behave in this way. I just can't understand how people like this can't see how their behavior is damaging the organization, not to mention their victims – the people in their organizations. I am not even sure how these managers got to the positions they occupy.

In another case where a manager like this came into an organization I watched with horror the plummeting of morale, the decline in trust of both management and people's peers, and the time that was wasted by people worrying that they would incur his wrath. If there was a way to minimize the commitment, effort, and quality of work you get from people, this is it. And, as in the cases described above, I wonder how these bosses would respond if they were treated in these ways.

THE DOWNRIGHT CRUEL BOSS

There is an annual competition to determine the worst bosses in the country. People vote, anonymously, by writing in stories about their bosses. I recently saw the results of one year's competition.

In one case, an employee's wife had a miscarriage at six months. This far along, a miscarriage is a very serious matter. The employee rushed his wife to the hospital, and after getting her settled, called his boss to say he wouldn't be in. The boss didn't seem to understand why the employee couldn't come to work, but the employee made it clear he wouldn't be in. Just two weeks later that same employee's father had a severe heart attack and wasn't expected to live. The employee accompanied his father to the hospital, and again called to report that he would not be coming in. Again, his boss couldn't understand why his employee wouldn't come to work. Later that day, the employee's father died. The next day he arrived at work to find that he had been fired for excessive unexcused absences!

In another case, an employee received a frantic phone call from his wife letting him know that his house was on fire. When the employee went to his boss to tell him he had to go home, the boss asked: "Is the fire department there?" The employee responded that they were, so the boss said: "Then you don't need to go home." When the employee protested that his house was on fire and he had to go home, the boss said: "Okay, if you go, you're fired." As it turns out, that was not necessary, the employee quit on the spot.

These stories are alleged to be true. While extreme, there are bosses who are cruel to their employees in many ways – sending a letter to the employee's home informing him he is laid off, not acknowledging successes but instead focusing on dissatisfaction, etc. How much commitment, loyalty, and hard work do you think these bosses get from their employees? I bet their people grudgingly do as little as they can to get by and move to other jobs at the first possible opportunity.

HUMANE LEADERSHIP

I have just spent a lot of time describing the inhumane and downright cruel ways in which managers can behave that eliminate any hope of getting the best from people. Now, how should we act? The answer is simple: First accept that we are all human, and behave in a humane way toward your employees. I mentioned what being human means above, so what does being humane mean?

It means that we understand the pressures that our people sometimes feel from outside the workplace. We understand, are sympathetic, and give them the slack they need to deal with those issues. We may even try to find ways that can mitigate the impact of outside situations.

In one place I worked we had a fund to provide temporary loans to staff who had financial problems. We couldn't do big loans, but they were big enough to help out – pay the rent this month for example. And, guess what, no one ever defaulted on a loan. It strengthened the bond between those who directly benefited from this program, and the people around them. There was a sense of caring that people really appreciated, and believe me, when we needed to call on them to do some extra work, or help with a special project, or... they were right there willing and anxious to help. A small bit of humaneness had a huge payoff in terms of motivating our staff. This is just one small example; there are multitudes of ways we as managers can demonstrate humaneness.

It means working with people in difficult circumstances by, for example, modifying their hours of work. You can offer a shorter workweek, coming in early or late and leaving early or late, letting them work part-time if need be, giving them an opportunity to telecommute – whatever works. The idea is to try to work with staff to ease the difficulties they might be having. This bit of humanity will strengthen their bond and commitment to you and your company.

I ounce even made a policy that women could bring their babies to work, as long as their presence did not disrupt or bother others. (Note, we didn't push them to do this, it was their option.) This also worked like a charm. We got a lot more work out of these employees than we would have if they were staying home, and they appreciated getting back to work to earn the income they needed.

It means treating people who make mistakes with dignity and support. This is such an important value in creating an environment in which people will do their best; I have devoted a whole chapter to it later in this book. So I will only briefly deal with it here in the context of the humane approach.

There is a level of tolerance, understanding, forgiveness, and learning that will amount to the humane way to treat people when they make a mistake. When someone makes a mistake, the humane way to respond is to be calm and supportive, accept the circumstance, and work with the person to understand what happened, and then set about fixing the problem. This approach is humane and it reassures both the person making the mistake and the people around him that they do not have to be afraid of incurring your wrath if you mess up. It is a comforting feeling for them, and it will cement your relationship, strengthen their loyalty, and motivate them to do their best.

It means avoiding temper tantrums at all costs. Never criticize or belittle a person in public. Show respect for every person who works for you.

When it becomes necessary to separate someone, such as a layoff, be as gentle as possible. Don't just leave people in the lurch, that is cruel, give them long lead times, provide outplacement assistance, help them find a new position, try as hard as you can to find another job for them in your organization, but if all else fails, make it possible for them to leave with dignity. This is the humane approach, and even though a layoff makes everyone feel badly or worry, your handling it in this way will reassure your people that if, God forbid, they ever found themselves in this circumstance they will be treated humanely. These good feelings will translate into their working as hard as they can for you.

We must begin by remembering that we are all only human. With this firmly in mind, use the humane approach to handling people's humanness. And, as the Golden Rule says, "Do unto others as you would have them do unto you." Don't treat people badly. If humanness and humanity are fundamental values of your organization, your people will give you their best, and by setting this kind of example, you will find that your subordinates will start treating each other in a humane way as well.

After all, isn't this the essence of a healthy family?

CHAPTER 2.5

I AM GOOD AT THIS BUT NOT THAT

In a family, each member is appreciated for his contribution to the family unit. A value of our organization is that we all should celebrate each other's strengths, use our strengths to fill in for other's weaknesses, and they will do the same for us.

IF YOU CAN'T DO WHAT I DO, YOU'RE A LOSER

I once had an accounting/financial person working for me who was really great at her job – highly skilled, very knowledgeable, and passionately committed to Scripps. Mary had one fault, however, that took me a long time to correct. She had no patience for anyone in the department who was not good at accounting, budgeting, or finances. Frankly, it was more than having no patience, she basically felt that people without these skills were incompetent and dumb and did not deserve to be in the positions they held even if their job did not explicitly require accounting and related tasks. She experienced no end of frustration, complained bitterly to me in private about how incompetent this or that person was, and how I should fire them on the spot. Of course, there were very few, if any, people in my unit (including me) who could even begin to meet her standard, so her complaints fell on deaf ears.

More seriously, she did not hesitate to make known to others in the group her feelings about another person, Ann. This caused others be nervous and fearful, wondering when they would be attacked.

BUT I AM GREAT AT WHAT I DO

Ann was extraordinarily creative and energetic. She had exceptional organizational, interpersonal, and leadership skills, all of which were essential to her job. Best of all, she was dedicated to Scripps, her heart was in it, and she really strove to do her best. But, you guessed it; she had virtually no accounting, budgeting, or finance skills. And, when I say *virtually no* skills I am being generous. Her brain was just not wired that way, and despite her own desire to learn, and my concerted efforts to help, it just didn't work. I even set up an Excel spreadsheet like a budget form that she only had to fill in for each of her projects, but that didn't work either. Of course, because of her excellence, she was an exceptionally valuable employee.

But, you can imagine how Mary felt about Ann. Even though Mary's creative skills extended to, but not beyond, setting up highly complicated spreadsheets and figuring out innovative ways to spend our money efficiently, when it came to the kind of skills at which Ann excelled, Mary's skills were not much better than Ann's financial acumen.

BEHAVIOR LIKE THIS HURTS THE WHOLE ORGANIZATION

In an organization this can lead to frustration and unhappiness not only for the individuals involved, but for everyone else as well.

Think about how one employee would feel about seeing another employee who he thinks is incompetent or at least not so smart being rewarded and/or promoted. Let's go back to Mary and Ann. Mary sees the type of work she does in her job as straight forward, obvious, and easy. On the other hand, Ann is just not wired to understand the work that Mary does. Mary sees this as weakness and feels Ann is just not with it. She is frustrated and angry that Ann is being recognized and rewarded for the work she does. At the same time, Ann is frustrated and angry that Mary is trivializing her accomplishments. The result is tension between the two employees. This is sensed by everyone else in the group and affects morale and collegiality. Sometimes people will take sides, creating friction between several people. Other times people will begin to fear that they will be next on Mary's hit list, and act accordingly, creating a political mess.

THEN THERE ARE TURF BATTLES

Sometimes situations like this can snowball into all-out war. If you are not vigilant, an employee who, because he does not respect another employee for the reasons we are discussing in this chapter, might try to take over or *move in* on the second person. For example, Mary thinks that Ann is basically incompetent because she has little if any financial skills. Mary might generalize this feeling to her image of Ann's work and feel she could do a better overall job than Ann. As a result, she may try to insert herself into Ann's area. Of course, Ann would resist, and the result would be infighting between the two. Or worse, suppose Ann is meek and as a result Mary is able to call the shots in Ann's area. Then, because Mary does not have Ann's skills, the level of excellence Ann would bring to the job on her own is degraded by Mary's interference.

BAD FEELINGS IMPACT THE WHOLE ORGANIZATION

Turf battles can spread through out the organization. What you end up with is at least two unhappy employees, and the overall performance of your organization is less than it could be. Efficiency, productivity, and morale suffer because, obviously, the involved employees are spending time on their problem that could be devoted to work. But others also waste time worrying or plotting to protect themselves. An environment of tension is created rather than the type of safe, positive, and self-actualizing, family, environment we are striving to create. Thus we are not getting the best from each of our employees, and the output of the group is less than it could be.

MANAGE STRENGTHS AND WEAKNESSES

So, what is the lesson that I had to teach Mary? Obviously, one must recognize that each individual has certain things that he is good at doing and certain other things that he is not good at doing. This is such an obvious point that you are probably thinking "dah." But you would be surprised how many people, including managers, think like Mary to one degree or another. They think that they are seeking *well-rounded* individuals. But, in fact, they are getting people (like me) who can do several things well, but none really great.

It is extremely important that we as managers do not allow this kind of thinking to infect our organization. It starts with you. You can't allow yourself to think that way about your subordinates. And, you must exercise leadership in getting your subordinates to recognize the value of the different skills, abilities, and knowledge that each person brings to the organization.

As a manager you must be able to identify each person's strengths and weaknesses, allocate tasks in the organization to maximize the use of each individual's strengths, and minimize the use of their weaknesses. In fact, this is fundamental to a successful organization. One person's strengths fill a gap left by another's weaknesses.

In the example above, once I got Mary to understand this concept, she was able to work with Ann to prepare the necessary budgets, etc. Believe me, this arrangement worked out exceedingly well. Mary was able to see and respect the complexity of Ann's job and her excellence. In turn Ann was able to see and respect Mary's excellence in what she did. The result was synergy – together they were greater that the sum of their parts.

Even more important, allocating duties to people based on their particular strengths actually sets them up to succeed, which is the fundamental goal we as managers should have for each of our employees. We want everyone in our little family to be successful. Thus, we must establish as a key organizational value that we all should celebrate each other's strengths and use our strengths to fill in for other's weaknesses. With this value permeating the workplace, people see that they can be successful in their jobs and will work as hard as they can to achieve and maintain their best and help others to be the best as well. They feel that they are contributing both to the organization and to each other, thus they feel secure in their jobs and feel very positive about their workplace, their peers, and their management. This is exactly the kind of environment we want to create to achieve our goal of getting the best from everyone.

CHAPTER 2.6

WE ARE NOT PERFECT

An organization where mistakes are valued as learning experiences rather than sins will be more like a family, will function better than it otherwise would, and people will be more likely to give their best.

In my younger years I was an apprentice cabinetmaker. My mentor was the perfect stereotype of an old-world cabinetmaker – a true craftsman. He was of German decent, probably in his early 60s, had gray hair, and always had a pipe in his mouth. His father, his father's father, his grandfather's father . . . were all cabinetmakers. He taught me a great deal, even though I did not end up having a career as a cabinetmaker. But, he taught me one lesson that has served me well throughout my whole life.

My first really big project, which he let me work on independently (with a lot of advice), was a 20-foot-long black walnut conference table. It really was beautiful when done, and I was so very proud – it was my first masterpiece. We had sent it to the finishing shop where about 10 layers of lacquer were applied. It shined and was perfect.

I was doing a few little finishing touches, and much to my chagrin, I accidentally dropped a chisel right in the middle of it making about a 3/8-inch dent. I was absolutely crushed – heartbroken. I had gone and screwed up my masterpiece. I was also petrified that my mentor would be really angry and possibly even fire me for my clumsiness. When I finally got the courage to tell him, he came over, walked around the table examining the dent, and said "hmmmm." Without saying another word he went over to his private toolbox and got out a little stick of something I had never seen before. He walked around the table again examining the flaw, and filled his pipe while doing so. Then he leaned over the table, lit his pipe and used his lighter to melt the stick and drip the melt into the imperfection. He filled the hole, used a piece of fine steel wool to smooth the surface, and applied a coat of furniture wax. Much to my amazement the dent was gone. You literally could not see it unless you knew where it was and looked closely.

He smiled, put his arm on my shoulder, and in his thick German accent said: "This was a good lesson for you. In your life you will make many mistakes, and it is the sign of a true craftsman to accept what you have done and proceed to fix your mistakes so that the final cabinet is as good as it otherwise would have been."

This insight has made a real difference in my life because I do tend to make mistakes – lots of them. This is not a "CYA" approach. Keeping my mentor's advice in mind, I admit to myself, and anyone else who is affected, that I made a mistake, accept it emotionally, and proceed to find a solution that makes things right again. In virtually every case during my career I have been able to find good solutions to problems. So, it works for me.

ACCEPT OTHER'S MISTAKES

It is great if one can apply this philosophy to one's self, but as managers who are trying to get the most out of people, it is vital to apply it when subordinates screw up. No one is perfect and can go though life error free. People will make mistakes. But, I, and maybe you, have had egocentric bosses who saw themselves as always being right, expected that from you, and flipped out when you did something that wasn't quite right. I know I was scared to death that I would incur my boss's wrath if I did anything wrong.

So, what do people who have bosses like this do? Here are a couple of strategies.

AVOIDING THE BOSS'S WRATH

One way to avoid the boss's wrath is to check with the boss about everything. This, to the egocentric boss, is probably great because he gets to prove his superiority. But it is really inefficient. Certainly as a manager, I didn't have time to deal with my people running to me with every little detail.

It also really slows things down. Once during my career I was essentially third in command. The deputy, who was between the big boss and me, insisted that everything go through him. The problem, of course, was that he was really busy and spent a good deal of time on travel. Thus, often it would take days, or more, for him to respond.

I have always had the philosophy that "the train is running down the track and can't stop to pick up every mail bag." That is why mailbags were put on posts, and as the train went buy, the bag was picked up with a hook

An even worse self-protective strategy used by employees caught in an environment where they are basically punished for making mistakes is that many will simply not do anything original, innovative, or risky: "If I only do the routine stuff, then I can't get into trouble." Unless you are operating a production line where each employee has a very specific, repetitive and unchanging job, this can be exceedingly detrimental to your organization.

CONSEQUENCES OF FEAR OF MAKING MISTAKES

Requirements such as those imposed by this deputy made the train stop and wait for him, so very little got done. When staffs are so paranoid about making mistakes that they run everything through the boss, essentially the train stops and has to wait for him to respond. So the business of the organization doesn't get done or at least not done in a timely manner.

Another truism is that when people feel it necessary to protect their livelihood by having the boss make every decision, the decisions tend to be less effective than they otherwise would be (although the egocentric boss would never admit to that).

The simple truth is that, in general, the boss is less knowledgeable about the employee's area than the employee. Thus the subordinate is in a better position to make good choices by virtue of the simple fact that he knows more than the boss.

When people adopt the "do only the routine" strategy it leads to stagnation. The organization remains static, and nothing really important gets done. There is very little improvement in operations or product quality. But at least the employee can't get in trouble, because he is just doing his job.

The most serious consequence is that pervading the organizational environment is a spirit of fear. This leads to low morale, and people wasting time trying to protect themselves. There is a lack of individual initiative, which is not only vital to the health of the organization, but also vital to the level of satisfaction of the employees. Do you think that people are doing their best under these conditions? Hardly!

WHAT SHOULD YOU STRIVE FOR?

It is very important the people under you feel safe and comfortable in confronting problems and mistakes in a straightforward and open way. They need to feel and believe in their hearts that if they come to you with a problem or mistake, you will not beat them up about it. Instead you will listen and work with them to fix the problem. Not only will this give your people a feeling of comfort and security, but it will help to bring problems to light before they damage the effective production of your organization's product. Also, participating in the solution to a problem will make employees feel more competent and effective in their jobs, which is a characteristic of self-actualization.

WHAT'S GOOD FOR THE GOOSE...

It is also important that they know that you are treating yourself in the same way that you are treating them. This goes back to the beginning of this chapter. You have to be able to openly admit your mistakes and enlist the assistance of your staff in finding solutions. Many managers will rebel against this approach, thinking that their staff will lose respect for them if they admit mistakes. But, quite the contrary is true. As long as you are treating them in a way that seeks solutions to problems, rather than retribution for them, they will feel closer to you, feel more comfortable dealing with their (and your) mistakes, and respect you more.

Even more important for building the kind of community we seek, if people see you behaving this way toward them and yourself, they will begin to treat their peers in the same way, which strengthens collegiality and a sense of community.

So, the essence of this chapter is that you establish a value system, which recognizes that no one is perfect (including you) and where problems and/or mistakes are dealt with in an open and problem-solving mode. Don't beat people up because they goof. Let them be human, and encourage them to admit that to themselves, to you, and to their peers. Doing this is very important to creating a work place family environment were everyone wants to do their best, and you get the most from them

CHAPTER 2.7

I HAVE A LIFE

Establishing the value that work and life are one helps to instill a sense of family and stimulates loyalty, commitment, and motivation in employees.

I don't know about you, but during the course of my career I found it difficult to separate my life at work from my life when I was not at work. Certainly, when I was at home I was very often thinking about work. Like most busy managers, I would bring work home from the office most nights (although I will admit that I didn't get much work done at home during the week) and on weekends. So at a minimum, I would be thinking about work when I was doing my work at home. But, it is also true that during many other times my mind would wander to matters having to do with my job. I just couldn't help it.

Similarly, when I was at the office I would often be thinking about my life outside the office. Sometimes I would even bring things to work on at the office that were related to my home life – kind of a reverse work at home. One can imagine any number of matters that can only be taken care of on a weekday. Further, just like there were times outside of work when my mind would wander to work-related matters, while at work my mind would often wander to home-related matters.

Does all of this make me a bad husband because my job occupies some of my time when I am off, or does it make me a bad employee because my home life occupies some of my time while I am at the office? My answer is an emphatic NO!

SEPARATING HOME LIFE FROM WORK LIFE IS IMPOSSIBLE

Many managers believe employees who do not spend 100 percent of their time during work hours fully focused on their jobs are not good employees. These managers are simply naive and unrealistic. It is essentially impossible to separate work life from home life; they are all one life. And trying to enforce standards that ignore this truism is a formula for disaster, at least in the context of our goal of getting the most from people. In fact, I contend that in order to create an environment where people give their best we should emphasize that time on the job is part of an integrated life where work and time away from work are really all one life.

These naive managers might scoff at me, saying "How can you possibly claim that you are getting the most out of people when you let them spend time at work, doing home-related things?" The answer is simply that while they are not doing home-related work, because of the supportive environment you have created, they will give you their all and want to do their absolute best for you. So, for the investment of a small amount of time for the employee to make a personal phone call, or fill out that mortgage form, or . . . or . . . or, you get a much more efficient and productive worker the rest of the time.

Let's say that you are the type of manager who expects people to have their noses to the grindstone 100 percent of the time. First and foremost, it is impossible to make this happen. You simply cannot control what is going on in someone's mind. The mind will wander to non-work-related things and it just cannot be controlled. In fact, I allege that if you make a rule that people can only focus on work-related matters during the workday, it is more likely their minds will wander. It is like the best way to get a teenager to do something is to tell him not to do it. So we cannot guarantee that people will have their minds totally focused all the time.

IMPOSING STRICT CONTROLS CAN BACKFIRE

Given that you can't control people's minds, you can certainly control their activities – right? You can make rules that there will be no personal phone calls, that no one is ever to have anything on his desk that is not work related, discussion among peers of non-work-related matters is forbidden, etc. And, you can even appoint a henchman to insure that these rules are followed. So have you won? No! In fact, you surely will lose more than you gain. First, and maybe worst of all, resentments will build up in people. Also, these kinds of restrictions will probably cause people to think more about non-work-related issues than they otherwise would or take more time off to deal with them.

There are many examples. One obvious one is the single parent who has a sick child. Suppose that person is prevented from calling the childcare center or the grandmother to check on the child's well being. Do you really think that the time lost in letting him make a phone call is more than the time lost while he is worrying about his child? Of course not. Once the concerns are satisfied with the latest information, the employee can stop worrying and focus on work.

What do you think that person will think about you if you create such a restriction? Not good thoughts. And, do you think that person will go out of his way to help when you need it – like coming in on the weekend, or working late? Not very likely. Or do you think that person will be taking work home on the weekends? I wouldn't bet the ranch on it. Or, in a more general sense, will that person really give his all to be the best that he can be for you? I don't think so. In fact, the most likely outcome is that the employee will choose to use vacation time to be with the child, rather than be isolated not knowing how he is. This cost you money, and nothing at all gets done.

WE WANT PEOPLE TO SEE WORK AS A POSITIVE PART OF THEIR LIVES

You get the idea, by ignoring the simple reality that people's lives are commingled; work with home and home with work, or by trying to make rules the deny that fact, you are really losing a great deal in employee loyalty, productivity, commitment, and motivation. It is a key value of the environment we are trying to create that we let people know we are comfortable with this duality. In fact, what we really want is for them to feel that work is a full and complete part of their lives. It is the difference between: "Damn, I gott'a go to work." and "Okay, off I go to the office, give me a call if you need me, see you this afternoon." We want people to want to come to work. This book is about how to create a workplace environment that does that, and it won't work if people feel that when they are at work they are completely isolated from the rest of their lives.

MORE FORMAL APPROACHES CAN ALSO BE USED

There are times when pressures at home do become so intense that more formal actions may be needed. Within the characteristics of the job that needs to be done, there are many ways to provide opportunities for people to respond to the issues at home – job sharing, telecommuting, flex time, etc.

For example, in the case of a chronically sick child it may be necessary for the parent to provide more continuous monitoring of the child's condition. In this case, a period of telecommuting may be the answer. I once had an employee who had a very old and feeble parent to care for. The parent did not need full-time monitoring, but also could not be left alone all day. The answer here was job sharing.

There are many ways managers can establish and promote the value that work and life are one. There is substantial benefit in doing this in terms of loyalty, commitment, dedication, willingness to go the extra mile, etc. It reinforces the sense that we are family, one big family including work life and home life. Conversely, ignoring this reality and/or rejecting this value in favor of one emphasizing that they are separate can backfire and have negative consequences on morale, loyalty, and productivity.

CHAPTER 2.8

WE ARE PROFESSIONALS

If professionalism is a fundamental value in your organization and you as the leader treat your people as professionals, they will give their best.

I have made it a point during my management career to treat all of my employees as professionals. I don't just mean the degreed analysts, supervisors, or technicians. I mean everyone in the family right down to grounds keepers and custodians. What I have found is that if you treat people as professionals, they will act like professionals. This is especially true of those people in the lower ranks. It is probably true because for most of them during their work lives they have been treated in the opposite way – like brainless automatons who had to be told what to do, how to do it, and when to do it. Employees should be given an opportunity to think for themselves, be independently responsible for their jobs, and have the freedom to do their jobs in the way they see fit. When they are treated in this way they feel good about their work life, have greater self-respect, and appreciate the trust that has been given to them. They, therefore, work harder and try to do the absolute best that they can.

CHARACTERISTICS OF PROFESSIONALS

A professional is a person who knows his job and more or less independently gets it done, usually with a high degree of excellence and often going well beyond his job description. Professionals are people who do not need to punch time clocks; they manage their own time. They put in more or less time depending on the needs of the organization, often working nights and weekends and probably taking off early sometimes. Although most like to come and go as they please, you can trust them to give you "a fair day's work for a fair day's pay" or maybe I should say "a fair year's work for a fair year's pay" since on a day-to-day basis their actual work time may vary. Nearly always, however, integrated over a year's time, their hours worked will exceed the number calculated for an eight-hour day, five-day week, etc.

LET PROFESSIONALS WORK WHEN THEY WORK BEST

Some employee's biorhythms may not resonate exactly with the normal eight-to-five workday. I have known many people who just do not get going until nine or ten in the morning. Similarly, there are those (and I am one of them) whose energy, concentration, ability to think, etc., are peaking in the early morning (like four or five a.m. or earlier) and hit bottom around two or three in the afternoon. In either case, do you think that you will be getting the best out of these people if you force them to come to work during the time when their biorhythms are at bottom? Of course, the answer is no.

As a matter of fact, it can be worse. Some people will just submit – drag themselves in early or wait until eight o'clock to come in. You're not getting their best for sure. They aren't as sharp as they would be if you let them work on their own clock. So, if you try to force a person whose biorhythms don't get going until nine o'clock to work eight to five, he will only be giving you seven hours of effective work. He is not functioning at peak between 8:00 a.m. and 9:00 a.m., so that hour is, for all intents and purposes, wasted.

Others will rebel and work against you. And others will simply leave your employ.

HOW BEST TO DESTROY A PERSON'S MOTIVATION

Let's turn to the example of the world's greatest purchasing agent. He was an early bird; he came in between five and six a.m. and got plenty of work done – especially working with vendors on the East Coast. By three o'clock, he was done, he was tired, and his efforts were ineffective, so he went home. This also made his commute easier. This schedule actually meant he was putting in nine or more hours per day.

He didn't report to me, but to a central purchasing office. One day his boss came back from a seminar on something like TQM and suddenly made a rule that everyone had to work 8 a.m. to 4:30 p.m. with a mandated one-half hour for lunch. Further, he went to great lengths to enforce this rule. My purchasing agent's job did not require that he be in during those hours. In fact, this new program had him putting in only eight hours per day. So, what happened to my world's greatest purchasing agent? His biological clock didn't work well on that schedule, and he felt he was being less productive. It also meant he was spending an extra one to two hours per day on the freeway. Frankly, he felt insulted because as he saw it he was not being treated as a professional and trusted to get the job done on his own time clock. So he retired early. This was a great loss to us all.

Now, don't get me wrong. I know that there are certain jobs that require being on duty during specific hours. Obviously, in these cases we can't be so flexible. Possibly, you should try to find someone whose biological clock works during those hours. But, unless there is some practical work-related reason why people have to be available certain specific hours, don't try to enforce arbitrary work hours

DO NOT MICROMANAGE PROFESSIONALS

It may come as a shock to you (or maybe not) that many managers, like my purchasing agent's boss, often treat even their higher-level employees as something other that full-fledged professionals. The term "micromanager" best fits managers like this. They want to dictate what a person's job responsibilities are, oversee how the employee does his job in detail, set arbitrary working hours, and make all kinds of work rules like those you might find in a highly structured union shop. Then they base their evaluations on how the employee complied with this micromanagement, rather than how good the employee's job got done. That is precisely what happened to our purchasing agent.

If you are attempting to micromanage your people, you are not treating them as professionals. You must assume they know how to do their jobs, and as discussed in chapter 2.3 on "Free to Be Me", everyone has a different way of doing things. More often than not, the more you try to interfere with professionals, the less productive they will be. When you micromanage professionals you frustrate them, stifle their creativity, and destroy their motivation. For example, I often did my most inspired work at 4 or 5 a.m. I did this work at home. If I had been told to work only while I was at the office, during regular working hours, the inspiration and motivation I had would have been lost.

DETAILED WORK RULES DON'T WORK

It is also quite dangerous to create detailed work rules. Professionals resent the implication that they don't, won't, or can't conduct themselves in a manner that is reasonable and ethical. This leads to resentment, anger, and a tendency to ignore the rules. Will we get more from our people if we try to get them to comply with a set of arbitrary rules or if we let them, within the practical constraints of the job, do their own thing? To me the answer is obvious – let them do their thing.

In fact, most often any attempt to create a set of rules will simply violate the freedom that professionals need to be most effective. As I have said repeatedly, a professional needs space to be able to manage his work life in the way that works best for him.

TREAT PEOPLE LIKE PROFESSIONALS

In the end, people who are treated like professionals will act like professionals. They will take pride in their work. They will want, for their own satisfaction, to do the best job that they can. Their rewards will come from knowing that they did their best, and their best was good. After all, isn't that we want?

To create an environment where you get the absolute best from your professionals you must instill a value throughout the workplace that recognizes and supports their need to be free to get the job done how, where, and when they want to. Do not enforce rigorous working hours. Do not punish them for taking an afternoon off now and then. Do not tell them how to do their jobs. Do not create detailed and specific work rules. Do not micromanage them. Do allow them to make decisions on their own. Do reward and recognize them for the quality of the work they do, for their commitment to your organization, their willingness to be there when they are needed, and their get-it-done attitude. Insuring that this value permeates your organization is fundamental to success in our goal of getting the best from people.

CHAPTER 2.9

I HAVE A FUTURE

People feel safe and secure in the knowledge that their family will always be there. When a value recognizing people's need to see that they have a future with your organization is pervasive, you will have low turnover and long-term employees who will give their best.

The most common reason that people change jobs is because of their supervisors. If you take this book seriously and create the positive value-based environment described herein, that reason for leaving should pretty much go away. However, many others do so because they want to advance their careers, and they see no future in their current job/organization. One objective of the approach I provide in this book is to stimulate longevity of employment. Much of the content provided here is focused on creating an environment where people will not only do their best, but want to stay with the organization just as the will always be part of their family. A major factor in keeping people is their belief that they will have a future within the organization. For just about everyone this means a feeling of safety and security in their current job. For some, however, having a future also means advancement in responsibilities and salary.

Responding to the latter group can be tricky because in most organizations, individual's growth is a long-term proposition. To convince people that they do have a future, they must be able to see that they have reasonable job security, that other employees in their group have and are moving up, that management supports career growth, and that many options are available to them to help prepare to move up.

SOME PEOPLE ARE SATISFIED WHERE THEY ARE

It should be noted that for some, having a future means job security without career advancement. These individuals reach a certain level, become very good at their jobs at that level, and are content to stay where they are. This is true when you as a manager are able to make them feel that what they do is important. You also may be able to help them to see what advancement might mean in terms of added responsibility, workload, stress, and, gently, the risk of the going beyond their capabilities (Peter Principle). These are not unmotivated people. As long as they feel appreciated, that they are in a supportive environment, and that they have long-term security, you will get their best.

SOME PEOPLE GET TOPPED OUT

There are also certain jobs where one advances to the top level in a specialty and becomes "topped out," but wants to continue advancing. In most organizations, continuing advancement for people in this situation would require them to change specialties. This is very difficult for some, and forcing the issue often results in failure.

An example: students in the MBA program I graduated from at UCLA were required to do a final project (much like a thesis) in a real corporate environment. The three of us in my team did a study of a large, well-known aerospace company. One of the problems we studied was engineers who were topping out. In order to respond to this, the company promoted many of their best engineers into management positions. Unfortunately, more often than not, these people were great engineers, but poor managers. As a result the failure rate was very high. There were problems attendant to poor management. Finally the company had a worse labor relations problem than they would have if they had only promoted those people who had real management training and skills. What do you do with a long-term employee – a great engineer who was promoted to management and who failed as a manager?

We recommended that the company create a parallel track for technical employees and management employees. The idea here is to recognize the value of the best engineers by broadening the salary range to be more equivalent to managers' salary ranges. This made sense because when it came down to it, those really high-end engineers were extremely valuable to the company, and in fact the managers' salary ranges were not that much higher than the engineer's anyway. This program worked because the best engineers, the ones who would have likely been promoted to management positions for retention purposes, could see the opportunity for continuing advancement doing what they were most comfortable with doing -- engineering. And, while it is true that eventually both managers and high-level engineers top out, the net result was a drop in turnover and an improvement in management. If you provide an appreciative, supportive and secure environment, employees will continue to find job satisfaction and give you their best.

This program worked for this company. It is also true that the University of California initiated a similar program that I participated in crafting, which remains successful to this day. However, every situation is different, and there are many ways to help people who are topped out. Individual growth programs like those described below are helpful, as are retraining for different jobs, internships, and more. The key here is that by making a concerted effort you are reinforcing to the other people in your group that you are committed to helping them have a stable and secure future.

ENCOURAGE AND SUPPORT INDIVIDUAL GROWTH

Within my organization virtually every one of my top-level unit heads started at lower levels and grew into their higher-level positions. They all, of course, had been with the institution for many years. But, much of their growth was a result of both their individual initiative and the considerable support that I provided.

There are three components to being a manager/boss who supports people's advancement. One is to encourage, and work with, the employee to develop a vision of where they want to go in their career. Next is being willing to provide and fund educational and other training opportunities consistent with the person's career goals. Last, and in my view the most important, is to give the employees a sense that you believe in them, you have confidence in their ability to develop and prepare themselves for advancement; and you are supremely confident that they can and will be successful both in achieving advancement and in their ability to do the higher level job. This last component can really make the difference. Your attitude about people can influence their own perception of themselves and their self-confidence.

HELP DEVELOP A VISION FOR THE FUTURE

In the process of career planning a couple of things can happen. One is that the person will simply seek continuing growth in his/her current field. The other is that a new direction will be identified. In either case, it is important to note a quote from Dwight Eisenhower: "Planning is essential, but plans are useless." What he meant by this, or at least my interpretation, is that thinking through a situation at the level necessary to construct a plan is very valuable. However, once you have developed a detailed set of steps that you think will get you where you want to be, almost without fail, as you move into the future, the actual steps you are taking will be different from the ones you planned.

In fact, I do not recommend that a detailed plan be developed. What is most important is to have a vision of the future. Quite the opposite from a detailed plan, this is a general image of where one wants to be in the future. Then let the future unfold. Life is full of opportunities, and as these opportunities present themselves, the temptation is to grab the first one. That could lead in a direction, which, in the end, will not be the most satisfying. With a relatively clear vision for the future, people can pick and choose those opportunities that most resonate with their vision and let the others go. It is very important that you as a leader help your employees to understand this. Otherwise, as time goes on, when not all those details in the plan come to fruition, it can be extremely frustrating. If on the other hand, the person sees movement toward his vision of the future, despite the details, he will feel successful.

ENCOURAGE AND SUPPORT EDUCATION/TRAINING

In terms of formal education/training, I made it a policy that I would fund and provide release time for any class or other training activity so long as it had some, even if remote, relationship to organizational needs and was consistent with employee's vision for his future.

I sometimes brought in speakers who had talks relevant to our business and encouraged staff to attend. These individuals do not have to be high-priced consultants. Most often they were people from other departments who could talk about their departments or some new policy/procedure they were implementing. This type of program not only helps the employees to advance their careers, but also helps them to do a better job in their current positions.

I encouraged reasonable attendance at professional society meetings. By reasonable, I mean probably only one per year and generally not in Antarctica (although I did have one employee, my diving officer, who went to Antarctica every year) or some other costly and difficult place to reach. I would also expect the employee to sign up for the training or educational activities that are often offered before and/or after the actual meetings.

SOME BOONDOGGLES AREN'T

Let me make one diversion here regarding my Antarctica comment. That was tongue in cheek. Sometimes activities that appear to be a boondoggle can turn out to be quite valuable. For example, I was fortunate enough to be able to attend, at institutional expense, a seminar entitled "The Disney Approach to People Management" at Disney World in Orlando, Florida. Well, you can imagine the comments: "Yea right, that's a lot of work, ha-ha-ha, I hope Mickey will give you some useful insights" and more. As it turns out this was without question the most valuable educational experience I ever had, and it had a great deal to do with my developing the approach that is the topic of this book. So when you are judging whether or not to approve attendance by one of your employees at a meeting or training program. you need to look closely at what the content is, not necessarily where it is.

I also found it very effective to use internships. This is a form of full-immersion, on-the-job training. During my career I had at least six different individuals participate in yearlong internships with me. During that time they would basically shadow me. Eventually, I would assign them projects or segments of my organization to give them practical experience, rather than just watching me in action. You may say: "That sounds expensive." Yes it costs money, but I found that for the most part my interns were able to shoulder a workload that, at least partially, made up for their salary, and in the end you get a more experienced and confident employee. Finally, in every case, these interns went on to higher level and responsible positions within the institution.

BELIEVE IN THEM

Lastly, the most important thing you can do is believe in your people, and let them know it. I know from my own personal experience that as one moves along the path of career development it can sometimes be discouraging. It seems like it is taking forever. There is a difficult class. Progress is slow because only one class can be taken at a time. Feelings of insecurity crop up. If you as a boss encourage people, let them know that you have confidence in them – you believe they have what it takes to succeed – it can overcome some of the frustration they feel and reenergize them.

Build people up, compliment them, help them to see other's success, and convince them that they can do it too. This level of personal caring coming from you as a boss can make all the difference for people and is just the kind of behavior from you that creates the environment where people want to do their best.

SAVE THE GOOD ONES

It is important that people in your organization feel secure about their future by seeing that you, as a manager, value them as persons, have confidence in their abilities (believe in them), and are committed to their success.

One set of circumstances that helps give people this feeling is how the manager handles others who seem to be having problems, or failing, in their current positions. Dealing with this is tricky because it requires the manager to make an assessment of the individual and determine if he is, or has the potential to be, a good employee who is just caught in circumstances that for some reason are not working for him. The opposite, of course, is that the person simply does not have what it takes and needs to move on to other opportunities outside your organization.

How do you handle these different circumstances? In the latter case, the answer is obvious. You let the person go in as humane a way as possible. In the former case, you do everything you can to provide opportunities for the employee to find something within your organization where he will be more successful. I want to emphasize that by saying, "Do everything you can," I mean that you need to be very proactive. Get involved with the person and try to get a handle on his strengths/weaknesses, then go out and look for a spot where he will fit in better. You might be surprised how the other people in your organization can distinguish between those who just don't have what it takes and those who have potential but are caught in a difficult situation. They can also see very clearly how you handle the ones who are savable and feel more secure because they know that if they ever get into trouble, you will be there to help.

Consider the following two examples.

The first involves a person who was hired from outside the institution into a department manager position in one of our divisions. He seemed well qualified and had a strong educational background. However, after just a few short months it became obvious that he was failing – I mean really failing. In particular, his staff just didn't like him. His management style turned people off, and despite his background he was not that well versed in the specific nature of the business done in that unit.

This manager did not report directly to me, but as the administrative head of the institution, it fell on my shoulders to fix the problem. I met with him several times to council him, but from the very first I made it clear that his chances of surviving in that position were poor at best. But, as I got to know him and see all of the positives he exhibited, I became more convinced that he was the type of person we needed. I looked for and found him a position in an active research group where the scientist who headed the group had had difficulty keeping people in a high-level support position. Knowing both, I thought that they might be able to work well together, and the employee had a good mix of skills, experience, and ability needed for the job. I got them together, and as is said, " . . . the rest is history." It turned out to be a marriage made in heaven. And working together, the employee and his boss built their group into one of, if not the, most successful at the institution.

The second example involves two long-term employees, a department manager and one of her top staff. Long story short, they just were not getting along. The conflict was intense, and it was seriously affecting the performance of them both. Something had to be done or one, or both, would quit, or the subordinate would get fired. Both were top-flight employees. Again, while they did not report directly to me, I proceeded with an intervention. I worked to calm the situation while I looked for another position for either one of them. One did come up, and I was able to place the staff person. By the way, it was a promotion. And, as in the previous case, she has been wildly successful.

As a manager, these two cases, and several others like them, gave me a sense of accomplishment and satisfaction better than any I have derived from any other accomplishment in my career. Also, it was good for the institution because I "saved" two really good employees who went on to make very significant contributions. Finally, as you know, there are no secrets in organizations, and others saw that management went out of its way to save good people, insuring their future. This image gave the other staff a sense of security and a feeling of trust in management, which is a key component of the environment that will stimulate the best from people.

So, in the end, as it would be in a real family those people who have gone as far as they want to, those who have gone as far as they can, those who are on a path to career growth, and those who seem to be failing, but who are worth saving, a manager must be able to create an organizational value where people perceive they have security and a sense that they have a future. They need encouragement, support, caring, and opportunity. It is very important here to emphasize that, as the patriarch in a family would, you as a manager must really want to provide all of this for your people and feel rewarded about doing so. Being genuine in providing a future for your people is another key component in creating an overall family environment where people not only give their best, but want to and feel good about doing so.

CHAPTER 2.10

I NEED TO KNOW

A key value in an organization is insuring that people know your expectations about how they do things or what they are doing.

Probably one of the most difficult and important issues for families and in organizations is communication. There are at least two kinds of information that one would like to communicate. First is the broad what's going on in the company: who is doing what, what opportunities exist for job advancement, new jobs, educational programs, and so on. The other is the information that is important to each individual's job: what are my boss's expectations, what do I do under this or that set of circumstances, what is/are my boss(s) thinking/expectations about policies, processes, and what should or should not be done and have those expectations changed.

The latter is by far the most important for the purposes of this book. That is not to say that broad communication is not important – it is. But difficulties or weaknesses in communicating broad information have far less consequences than those for communicating job-related information. Thus, I will only briefly discuss the former and emphasize the latter.

BROAD ORGANIZATION-WIDE COMMUNICATION IS TOUGH

The last thing I want to do in this book is to express hopelessness. However, my own experience after thirty years of trying to solve this problem is that nothing really works that great for broad, organization-wide communication. I assure you this is not from lack of trying. I have spent tens and tens (and probably hundreds) of thousands of dollars attempting to achieve a high level of information transfer. It is true that if people generally don't know what is going on in the organization, about new policies and procedures, what opportunities may exist for them, etc., it can lead to frustration. I have tried newsletters, broadly distributed memos, e-mails, big all-hands meetings, smaller talk-with-the-boss meetings, and unit head meetings.

Newsletters and memos have limited value. They are expensive, and I have found that after awhile fewer and fewer people actually read them. Let's face it, it is pretty near impossible to make a corporate newsletter or formal memos interesting and exciting to read.

Large meetings are problematic as well. First of all, it is difficult to get full participation in large all-hands meetings. Even *mandatory* meetings don't get everyone. So, the people who don't come to the meetings don't get the information, and it is passed along from those who did attend only sporadically. Inevitably, at some later date when something happens that was discussed at the meeting, those who did not attend would come out of the woodwork with the lament: "Why wasn't I informed about this?"

Smaller meetings (like my senior staff meeting – Family Council) seemed to work better. But, there just isn't time to cover hundreds of people with a bunch of small meetings. Relying on attendees at small meetings to pass along the information they picked up to others in their group is overly optimistic. In most cases it doesn't get done.

I have often fantasized that if I could only create a communication system that worked as well as the grapevine I would achieve nirvana. I have had no such luck. But, that does not mean we should give up. Some people do get the information. And, for those who cry: "Why was I not told about that?" we can fall back on: "It was in the newsletter, memo, e-mail, or discussed at the meeting."

COMMUNICATION OF JOB-RELATED INFORMATION

Certainly, failures of communication of broad organization-wide information can lead to frustration among the staff, but I have found that as long as we keep trying, people might complain, but it really isn't a major morale problem. However, when a manager fails to communicate his expectations, or changes in those expectations, about a person's job, then punishes the employee for not behaving in accordance with those expectations, it creates extremely serious problems. This management error can have a very negative impact on employee morale, motivation, loyalty, commitment, trust, etc. In other words, all of the characteristics we want to see in our employees are impacted and can sometimes be extinguished. This leads, of course, to their not giving their absolute best.

MISHANDLING A FAILURE TO COMMUNICATE CAN BE DEVASTATING

Have you ever had this happen to you? You have been doing your job for a very long time. You have freedom and the trust of your bosses to do what you are doing, and you have always done a great job, as measured by consistent compliments and superior evaluations. At some point, a new manager comes along – your boss, your boss's boss, your boss's boss's boss. You're working along, doing your job as always, when one day, this new boss, or one of his operatives, comes to you and reads you the riot act because you are doing this or that wrong, " . . . you screwed up again." Of course, your answer is "This is the way I have always done it. I didn't know that you had changed the way you wanted it done. I will from now on . . ." but by that time he has already stomped out of your office.

If you have had this experience, how did you feel? I know I, and others I have interviewed who have been through it, felt bad, scared, angry, betrayed, hurt, confused, de-motivated, etc.

Was something done wrong? Yes, most definitely, but not by the employee, by the boss. How was the employee to know that things had changed if no one told him? To beat someone up in this kind of circumstance is not only bad management, it is fundamentally wrong and cruel (inhumane) and definitely not the family way of doing things. This is just the kind of behavior that destroys the workplace environment we want to create – the environment that promotes the best performance from employees. I am sure you would be surprised at how many managers thoughtlessly error in this way. In fact, this chapter grew out of a recent incident where I observed just exactly this kind of behavior from a high-level manager.

EVERYONE KNOWS

The environment is broadly affected, not just for the direct victims, but others as well. Incidents like this are not kept secret. As I said above the grapevine works great: "Wow! Did you hear about what happened to Jimmy? That new boss is really a . . ." and on and on the gossip goes, generally making the story worse as it passes through each person.

So, what is the outcome? Mostly, people get paranoid. They don't want this to happen to them. They go to greater lengths to CYA, and in particular they are afraid to do anything creative for fear that it will be wrong. As a result things don't get done as quickly as they otherwise would and productivity goes way down. There is a chilling effect on the organization. Collegiality is lost. People no longer want to be at work. They lose trust in management. Their motivation is reduced. They no longer strive to do their best; they strive to do what they think you want them to do. This is suboptimal. If it is seen as happening often, people start looking for new jobs. Why would they want to work in a place where they get beat up for doing what they have always been rewarded to do? This was precisely the tragic impact that the incident I mentioned above had on that organization.

IT'S A FAILURE OF COMMUNICATION

What really happened? There was a failure of communication. The boss wanted something done in a certain way, but didn't tell the employee. But, the real mortal sin was that he then punished the employee for doing it wrong, rather than saying, "Jimmy, you did a great job on this . . . let's try doing it this way next time." A manager who provides this kind of feedback will be trusted and get the best from people.

By the way, the example above blames this problem on a new boss who changes things coming in. It is important to note that bosses who have been around are often guilty of the same sin. They can also decide that things should be done differently and forget to let people know.

A related, but possibly more common mistake that occurs with bosses is as follows: The employee is subjected to his annual performance evaluation during which he is marked down for failure to do certain tasks that the boss wants done. It turns out that no one told him things had changed. The impact on the employee may be even worse because review time is very stressful.

Making this type of management error must be avoided at all costs. It can be one of the most devastating problems to the successful creation of an environment where we get the best from our employees. So, how do we avoid it?

AVOIDING THIS ERROR

The first answer is always "the job description." HR people and organization development consultants will put this first on the list. As I discussed in the "How Do I Fit In" chapter I really am not convinced that formal job descriptions are the end all and be all. I, personally, as a manager have always been frustrated with the job description process. This book is about how to manage professionals. They really don't need to have a lengthy document containing every detail of their job. In fact, they often resent it when someone tries to do this. They need to be given latitude and independence.

What is vitally important is that when you want to change something, either a way of doing something (i.e., a procedure) or add or subtract from the job, you tell the affected employees when the change is made.

But, suppose you forget. As managers we are all busy. I know that in the intensity of my day-to-day work life, I forgot things all the time. So if you do fail to communicate a change or a new task to an employee, it is critically important that if he doesn't do it the new way, you do not punish him. Don't make the employee pay for your mistake. Instead if you see that something is not being done the way you want, go to the employee and say: "Jimmy, you're doing such a great job, but you know I forgot to tell you that we want to do this now . . .Thanks." Guess what? Jimmy, in 99 percent of the cases, will say: "Okay, boss, no problem, thanks for telling me."

And, this is the answer. Sit down with the person and discuss what you want or the change that is being made. Complicated and detailed revisions to job descriptions don't achieve the positive results that a personal conversation will.

What a difference! You will get it done the way you want and you made a stronger bond with your employee. Now everyone will say: "Wow, our boss is so cool, he supports us, gives us guidance, lets us know how he wants things done, and always congratulates us on the good things we do." This, of course, strengthens the kind of environment we want to create.

To sum up, broad communication of information about what is going on in the organization is quite important, but achieving significant penetration is very frustrating. All of the methods one can think of fail in one way or another. Despite this, managers should never give up. Far more important is to establish a value in the workplace environment that we strive to communicate to employees what our expectations are regarding their job. And, of greatest importance: Don't beat people up for not doing what you want if you haven't told them what you want or how you want it done.

CHAPTER 2.11

WE HAVE FUN

Families that play together stay together. A workplace where having fun is valued is one where people will want to be.

An old cliché is: "laughter is the best medicine." There is nothing like a good laugh or even a light chortle or a sincere smile to ease tension, work around a difficult subject, give a frustrating situation a more positive spin, lighten a mood, make a bad situation more tolerable, or just have a little fun. A joke, even a bad one, can help people to forget their problems and move on to solutions.

I don't know about you, but I can't function if I don't try to turn difficult situations into a laughable circumstance. If you examine the material that the best comedians use, it becomes clear that the funniest things involve lighthearted perspectives on real life. For me, this real life source of jokes is often myself. I need to laugh at myself, often to help me to overcome guilt or self-abuse for mistakes or just to make difficult situations easier to accept.

For example, I got to a point where my e-mail was truly oppressive. I was getting well into three digits of mail every day. So, I told people that from now on, the only e-mail I would read was the jokes. People, of course, knew I was just kidding, but the chortle helped me to face up to my e-mail overload and probably helped others whose e-mail was also out of hand to deal with their situation as well. And, to top it off, I started getting less e-mail and more jokes.

MAKING YOUR WORK FUN

Making fun out of difficult or challenging situations is one of the best ways to keep morale at a high level in the workplace. But, it is also possible to look for fun in the content of one's job. For some it may be fun to solve a difficult problem. For others it may be fun to generate new ideas. Having fun doing things gives people a desire to do more of those things. If you are having fun doing something, you will tend to spend more time thinking about that thing, whatever it may be. Not only will you spend more time thinking about it, but also your thoughts will be occupied by how to do it better. If you are having fun at work, then you will want to be there.

In all my years as a manager I have never found a person who could not find some aspects of their job fun. I might have to help them, but there is always something. For example, I was called upon to do a lot of public speaking. I would go all over San Diego with my talk about Scripps. I really had fun doing that.

But, even if there wasn't something already in the job that was fun, I could almost always find some task or set of tasks that needed to be done, that the person could have fun with, and that I could assign to them. Everyone wants to enjoy their work, and I have found that they really appreciate my encouraging them, or even helping them to find fun in their jobs.

A wonderful woman who was one of our purchasing agents makes for a good example. Purchasing can be drudgery, and as it happens the purchasing agents at Scripps actually reported to another unit outside of the institution. At that time, the head of purchasing to whom she reported was a true tyrant. There had to be something for her to do that wouldn't irritate her boss. The answer was a beautiful saltwater aquarium we had in our office. She took charge of the aquarium, and she had fun, real fun taking care of the fish. She looked forward to coming to work so she could look after "her babies."

MAKE SAYING "NO" EASIER

When I was assistant dean in the engineering school at UCLA a serious financial problem came up. About 2/3 of the fiscal year had gone by and my projections indicated that essentially all of the departments were close to running out of money. We had to sharply curtail their spending and use school-wide money to bail them out, so there was none left for special requests from departments and faculty. I started a "No More Mister Nice Guy" campaign. Someone had given me a "No More Mister Nice Guy" coffee cup, and I obtained a package of "No More Mister Nice Guy" sticky notes. I brought my coffee cup to all of the meetings I attended. I used the stickies to remind people, in a somewhat lighthearted way, that we were out of money, at least for the rest of the year. All requests for funds, except the most urgent, were turned down with a little "No More Mister Nice Guy" sticky affixed. It worked – special requests basically stopped and although we all had to do without for a while, everyone seemed to accept the reality and go with the idea.

The "No More Mister Nice Guy" campaign was a way of saying no in a lighthearted way. One affect was that many people stopped asking, so it was not necessary to say "No" as often. Saying "No" is always hard; at least it was for me because I always wanted to help people who had needs to make their programs work. That was my mission and my reason for being there. It is also true that saying "No" can generate anger, hostility, and envy. But at some point it becomes necessary, and if we find a more fun way to do it, it makes it easier and helps to quell the bad feelings.

At one point at Scripps we were in the process of occupying a new building. This involved reshuffling many people. For any of you who have had to do this, you know that it can be a wrenching, disruptive, and very expensive process. Everyone who is moving to a different location always wants to configure the new space to suit his or her needs (or wants), even if the space is in a brand new building. Of course, those who were moving into old space that was vacated by people moving into new space were even more demanding.

I had weekly meetings with my facilities and space management staff and the building occupants who were being moved. We used these meetings to give updates on the status of the moves and to hear requests or problems from the people moving.

Clearly the volume of requests was more than we could accommodate either financially or with the manpower we had. Therefore, I had to prioritize, which meant that some people would not get their requests satisfied, at least not right away. So I had to say no fairly often. A couple of times, projects that I had approved were scheduled to be undertaken the following Tuesday. For one reason or another these projects did not get done. All of a sudden it became a joke that if your project was scheduled for Tuesday, it wouldn't get done. So we picked up on that and from then on, whenever I decided to put someone's request on the "Tuesday List" it meant that that project was deferred or possibly would not be done. I can't say that being put on the Tuesday List made people happy, but at least they were still on a list, we could all smile a little about it, and it was much easier than giving a flat "No."

MAKING THE BEST OUT OF BAD SITUATIONS

Sometimes the stress of even the direst circumstances can be relieved with a little fun. One year at Scripps we were facing very serious budget cuts. Someone put up signs around the office that said: "The light at the end of the tunnel has been turned off." This certainly didn't solve the budget cuts, but as far as morale goes it was a lot better than listening to the doomsayers. In fact, often when people are faced with problems or uncertainty, they tend to imagine the worst possible outcome. One way to offset this tendency is with levity.

Sometimes there is real "pain and suffering" that can be mitigated by doing our best to laugh. When the budget cuts did hit it became necessary to eliminate an administrative assistant position (fortunately through attrition) from my already overwhelmed public affairs unit. This was a real blow to them because, as you might have guessed, the workload didn't go away. I was completely sympathetic with their problem but despite passionate begging on their part, I wasn't able to help. So, what did they do? They created a virtual administrative assistant. One person sewed a face and head, and others stuffed rags, etc. into stockings, a pants suit and a blouse. They named her Lois and sat her at the administrative assistant's desk, saying they had to hire her, despite her lack of experience, because she worked cheap. This really helped all of us to get through these difficult times and reminded me every time I walked through their office how much they needed more help.

The story has a happy ending. When I finally got some extra money, the first cut restoration was for the Public Affairs Office, and, believe it or not, the real person they subsequently hired was named Lois.

(I should also add that when I retired I no longer had the support of an administrative assistant, so I hired Lois. She is sitting right here in my office with me.)

MAKE FRUSTRATION EASIER TO HANDLE

Levity can come in handy to dampen people's frustrations. We all get frustrated on the job from time to time. On one occasion, we were in the middle of construction on a new building. We were having grave problems with the plans that the architect had prepared: incorrect specifications, alignments from one drawing to another didn't match, just plain errors, etc. We had just about every problem imaginable that could be had with a set of building plans. In the meantime, the contractor we hired was equally incompetent. There were long delays, things built wrong even when the plans were correct, cost overruns, etc – you get the picture. Trust me, we were all really frustrated.

We were too far into the project to fire the contractor, and the architect had already been paid for much of the work. We basically couldn't do anything except "grin and bear it." So we did. Someone suggested we burn the contractor and the architect in effigy. One person made some little paper figures that we named after the architect and contractor. Another made a fancy urn for the ashes, and we set them up in the office to remind us that, in the end, we would get our revenge. While I must admit we never got around to the actual burning ceremony, we had a lot of fun with the whole idea and it made it a lot easier to get through the situation.

(One side note, we ended up suing the architect and got a $900,000 settlement, but, you guessed it, the lawyers got it all. Most people get a chuckle out of the reality that most of the time the lawyers end up getting the money, but to date I have still not been able to make a joke out of this one.)

HAVE FUN EVEN IF THERE ARE NO PROBLEMS TO LAUGH ABOUT

Over the years there have been many circumstances where I was able to use humor to reduce the impact of problems and bring people closer together. But, you can still have fun, even when there are no big problems. For example, we had a tradition in my unit heads meeting – Family Council. Each week I would bring the worst joke I could find and tell it at the end of the meeting. These were usually "groaners," which were probably more fun than real jokes.

I often would make fun of myself, especially when I screwed something up. That was the best way for me to get through it, and it set the tone for others to spend less time beating themselves up and more time laughing at themselves. And, this is really the secret.

You can even make good things better doing fun things. Every ten years the National Academy of Sciences ranks the research and teaching programs at academic institutions around the U. S. In the early 1990s, as I will mention in the chapter on pride, Scripps was ranked No. 1 among all oceanographic institutions in the country. That, of course, is a great honor, not only for the institution, but all the people in it. So, rather than have a dignified reception to celebrate, we had a pep rally. We had pennants made up with the Scripps logo and "WE'RE #1" printed on them. We even had cheerleaders. It was great fun, except possibly for the stodgiest. In fact, one curmudgeon made the comment that not only did he not think Scripps was number one, but there were no oceanographic institutions that were number one – the best was probably five or six!

SET THE TONE

I am by no means a comedian, nor do I have the creativity to think up things like the pep rally, the "Tuesday List", Lois, etc. You need not be either. All of the examples I mentioned above came not from me, but from people around me. In truth, after a while, I didn't even have to look for jokes for Family Council. My staff would send them to me. Basically, as the leader of your group what you have to do is set the tone. Make it clear that it can be fun to be at work, we encourage people's sense of humor, that we want to take the time to laugh, that even in the most difficult of times, a laugh, a chortle, even a smile can chase away the sourpusses and the doomsayers. The best part of being a family is having fun together.

Our goal as managers is to create an environment where people give their best. People give their best when they want to come to work, where they can have enjoyment and fun. Having fun in the workplace is a key component of the environment we want to create. As managers, we don't have to be comedians or cruise directors. All we have to do is to set a tone that welcomes fun, laughter, and good feelings. You will be surprised at the senses of humor that will come out of the woodwork and make things fun for everyone.

SECTION THREE

MOST
IMPORTANT
VALUES

The values described in this section are essential to the success of this program. These, along with those already described, make up the workplace family that motivates our employees to do their best

CHAPTER 3.1

WE ARE PROUD

Most people are proud of their family. In organizations where pride is a value, everyone in the group feels good about what they do, where they do it, and whom they do it with. This motivates them to do their best.

Remember the Seven Deadly Sins: lust, gluttony, greed, sloth, wrath, envy, and pride?

A member of our faculty at Scripps, one of my favorite people ever, commented when the subject of the Seven Deadly Sins came up that he was qualified in all seven and distinguished in four!

While I will not comment on my own qualifications in this area, I may be committing a mortal sin in this chapter. I contend that pride is not a deadly sin, not even a sin; it is one of the most important factors in creating an environment where people give their best.

I have never quite understood why pride is seen as a sin. This is probably because I never really looked into what pride means as used in Christian literature. Here is a discussion of pride I found on the Wikipedia:

In almost every list Pride is considered the original and most serious of the seven deadly sins, and indeed the ultimate source from which the others arise. It is identified as a desire to be more important or attractive than others, failing to give compliments to others though they may be deserving of them, and excessive love of self (especially holding self out of proper position toward

God). Dante's definition was "love of self perverted to hatred and contempt for one's neighbor." In Jacob Bidermann's medieval miracle play, Cenodoxus, Pride is the deadliest of all the sins and leads directly to the damnation of the famed Doctor of Paris, Cenodoxus. In perhaps the most famous example, the story of Lucifer, Pride was what caused his fall from Heaven, and his resultant transformation into Satan. Vanity and Narcissism are prime examples of this Sin. In the Divine Comedy, the penitent were forced to walk with stone slabs bearing down on their backs in order to induce feelings of humility.

Wow! It looks like I am treading on thin ice. Not only is pride one of the Seven Deadly Sins, it's the worst! Possibly I can avoid being "...forced to walk with stone slabs bearing down on my back..." by sincerely saying, with the greatest of humility (doing it with humility may give me some modicum of atonement), I advocate that as managers we should make every effort to have our employees feel proud of what they do, where they do it, and the people they do it with.

A MILDER GENTLER PRIDE

Perhaps I will be safe because I am suggesting a milder, gentler, and more humble form of pride than is described above. Not the overly narcissistic form of perverted love of self that is manifested by hatred and contempt for our neighbors contemplated by Dante. That is the type of pride that stimulates the ruthless kind of vicious competition I decried in the chapter on office politics. Instead I advocate a type of pride that stimulates us to be the best, but not at other's expense. This type of pride makes us feel good, not just about ourselves, but about the things and people around us.

PRIDE IS EVERYWHERE

I worked my way through college on yachts. The first one I worked on was a 55-foot cabin cruiser called the *Heathco*. This was where I first was exposed to the power of pride in motivating maximum performance. The *Heathco* was not the biggest yacht, nor the most opulent, in the marina. But the skipper insisted that the boat had to be perfect at all times. What that meant was that everything was super-clean, even the engines had to be wiped of oil and dirt after every cruise. The varnish was always perfect, as were the teak decks. Inside, everything was spotless even down to under the bunks in the crew's quarters. I was so proud of that boat. We worked so hard to make it perfect, and it was. I wanted more than anything to keep it that way, because I was proud. I did my best to make it so.

Have you ever been to Disneyland or Disney World? You probably have, but have you ever taken the time to really look at the details? I have, and everything is perfect. It is super-clean all of the time. Every structure looks like it is brand new. The paint is fresh, the streets look like they have never been used, the landscaping is vibrant, and the trains look like they have just gotten out of the yard from refurbishment. I could go on and on because I pay attention to those things.

In the chapter "I Have a Future" I mentioned that I had the privilege of participating in a conference on "The Disney Approach to People Management." One of the things I learned is that a big part of the motivation of people in the Disney organization is that they are proud of how everything is kept perfect. They are proud and that makes them work harder to keep things that way, and as a result, they are.

Because I experienced the motivational effect of pride on *Heathco*, I intuitively knew that it was important, but it was the conference at Disney World that really brought into focus the power of pride in motivating people to be the best.

Look around, pride is everywhere, and it doesn't seem to be ruining the world. We are proud of our sons and daughters who are successful, we are proud of our college's football team (if it wins), we were proud when we were first to land a man on the moon, there is even a song: "Proud to be an American." The examples are endless. Being proud of something gives us a good feeling, makes us smile, and often celebrate. When one accomplishes something and is proud of that accomplishment, it gives him incentive and motivation to do more of the same. Were we wrong to be proud to be part of Scripps Institution of Oceanography when the National Academy of Sciences ranked Scripps No. 1? Of course not. Did it make me, and all of the people around me, want to keep doing our best to keep Scripps on top? You bet it did.

So, I have experienced it myself and have seen how important pride can be. We see that pride is everywhere. Now I hope that I can convince you that instilling pride in your people can strengthen their sense of family and make a profound difference in how they perform and in their motivation to be the best.

PRIDE IN WHAT

Let me once again emphasize that instilling feelings of pride in your employees is an essential part of the environment that stimulates them to do their best.

Pride in who I work for, or pride in my company, is the first and most important. It is having the feeling that where you work is a good place, that it makes a product that is good, and that it is one of the best, or the best, in their industry. It is feeling good when you tell someone where you work.

Pride in what I do is the feeling that my job, and especially how I do it, makes a difference and is important in helping to achieve the things that make you proud to be part of the company. It is being recognized for work you have done. It is a feeling that you stand out in your profession. It is knowing that you are doing the best of the best.

Pride in those around you is the feeling that the people you work with are also the best. It is feeling good about their successes. Being glad and happy when one of your colleagues is recognized for accomplishments because their achievements are part of the overall package that makes you proud to be a part of your company.

Feeling that your company is the best, the products it produces are the best, your contributions to making those products are the best, and the people you work with are the best is not bad, and it is not a sin. It is rewarding. It gives people meaning in their lives, and it makes them want to do their best to keep having those feelings. It is key in what makes people want to come to work and be a part of the organization they are in.

GIVE FEELINGS OF PRIDE TO YOUR PEOPLE

As managers, we are fundamentally responsible for instilling these feelings of pride in our employees. Where do you start? Well, for one thing you have to "walk the talk." You have to have that feeling of pride at all of the levels mentioned above.

It starts with pride in the company. If you don't feel it, then you probably should not be a manager in that company. You really have to talk it up. Use every occasion that you can to say, "I am really proud to be a part of this company" for this or that reason(s).

I have been sitting here trying to think of some type of legitimate business where it would not be possible to find any reason to be proud to be a part of it. It ain't easy – try it. I just can't think of any. In fact, it is much easier to find reasons to be proud of just about any endeavor. As a manager it is your job to find those aspects of your business that can make people proud. One easy one is to be the best of whatever business you are in and the products you produce. Your widgets are the absolute best produced anywhere. There are many others: we are proud to be environmentally sensitive, we are proud that what we do helps people, we are proud that our company has a generous philanthropy program. The list goes on and on. In fact, although I use the term "legitimate business" above, I bet that many people in illegitimate businesses often feel pride: we are the best hackers around, we just pulled off the impossible heist of a Rembrandt, etc.

Producing the best products really requires that the people who produce them do the best in their jobs. Which leads to the next element – pride in the work you do. When a person sees that his contribution to producing whatever you produce is important in helping that product be the best there is, he can't help but feel pride. People can be proud of the job they do; you just need to let them know that you are too: "The job you did on that really makes me proud" and mean it. People will see that you are speaking from the heart and will be infected with that same level of pride. To me it really isn't difficult.

Finally, helping people to see how everyone in the organization contributes to making your products the best helps people to feel pride about the people they work with. Again, as a manager, you need to be proud of your whole group, then express that to them: "Wow! Look what we accomplished together. I am really proud of how you all worked together . . . you are all superstars!"

Also, help people to be proud of their peers when they do something good. The way you do this is to talk it up: "We should all be proud of the way Jimmy handled that irate customer . . . he made us all look good" or "I am really proud of this new publication that Sandy put together, it is really great. I will, and I am sure you will, be proud to hand it out to people."

So, a key component of the environment we are seeking is a sense of pride that permeates the employees under you. And, basically, the way you create that is to see the characteristics of your organization that you can be proud of, feel it yourself, and openly and enthusiastically express it to your people.

CHAPTER 3.2

WE REJECT OFFICE POLITICS

Family members don't play political games with each other. A principle value of an organization should be that office politics will not be tolerated.

This is one of the most important issues of all those I have discussed. If you don't remember anything else I have written in this book, remember this chapter. Office politics are the most destructive of all maladies organizations suffer. It is impossible to obtain the best from your employees if you allow politics to infect your organization. An organization where office politics occur is guaranteed to be less efficient, less productive, and less effective and will produce a much lower quality product than any organization where politics do not exist. When political wars occur in an organization there are at least one "winner" and two or more losers – the looser(s) in the war, and the organization. I call these wars the "Washington Syndrome" because it is my observation that virtually all of the government bureaucracies in Washington, D.C. are hotbeds of office politics. (My apologies to those of you who work in Washington, and do not suffer this malady – I am happy for and congratulate you.)

WHAT ARE OFFICE POLITICS

What do I mean by office politics? I am sure that most of you who are reading this book either have been, or are currently, victims of office politics. They are generated by a pervasive atmosphere of perverted competition. Brutal competition is probably a better characterization. What it amounts to is people trying to build their career at the expense of others. There is backstabbing and plotting against one another. Politics arise when people are so desperate to get ahead that they are willing to do just about anything (except just doing the best job they can) to anyone to make the boss think they are better than others. These people, in my opinion, are generally individuals who, either consciously or subconsciously, believe they do not have, or in fact do not have, the skills, ability, knowledge, intelligence, or whatever else it takes to be successful on their own merits. Rather than work hard and do their best, they use these tactics as a shortcut to advancement. As a result they stoop to destroying, as best they can, their peers. By this I mean they do everything they can to criticize other's work and/or find fault in any characteristics of other persons in the organization. They will bad mouth people both within the group and to their managers. They question others' performance, denigrate others' work products, and find, usually in hindsight, ways to point out deficiencies in others' work. They will engage in sabotage to create the appearance of poor performance of others. They belittle people and boast of their own superiority. They will cultivate alliances against other individuals. The fundamental goal is to make them look better than everyone else. The belief is that by sabotaging everyone else so they will look bad, the perpetrator will stand out as performing far better than everyone else.

I used the word "infect" above. Office politics is an infection because it spreads. If one or more people within the group play this game, others who otherwise would not must also play in order to survive. Rather than just trying to do the best at their jobs, they must spend time defending themselves and/or fighting back. Or they just isolate themselves and play as low a profile as possible.

OFFICE POLITICS ARE PERVERTED COMPETITION

Many will argue that competition is good and motivates people to do their best. They will hold sports up as an example of how competition stimulates people to do their absolute best and beyond. There is no argument with this observation. However, there is a profound difference between competition in sports and competition in the workplace. Sports have strict rules, and there are referees to make sure the rules are followed. But office politics perverts competition. There are no rules or umpires in a workplace environment; it is "every man for him self." There is no regulation of what you can and cannot do to each other in this maniacal drive for advancement and power. As a result, the competition can be vicious and cruel and there is nothing to stop or control this behavior. Thus, people get seriously hurt and not a pulled muscle or sprained ankle that athletes suffer. It is the kind of hurt that ruins peoples' lives and often that of their families as well. So this kind of poison must be avoided at all costs.

EXAMPLES

The first time I really became aware of this phenomenon was not in an office setting. I was an undergraduate student at UCLA taking a chemistry class that included several premed students. At that time medical school was extremely hard to get into, with only the top of the top of the classes accepted. So it was in individuals' interests to see their fellow students be less successful. I was shocked to see students doing everything they could to make their peers fail. They would sabotage each other's lab experiments, claim that their opponents were cheating, and every other thing you could imagine to get ahead. How naive I was. Fortunately I was only an engineering major, and I was not a threat to the premeds so I was not subjected to this abuse.

I really didn't get it until I observed, and was a victim of, this behavior in other contexts. There have been many over the course of my career, and each time I observed, or even had to face, office politics in action I became more convinced of its destructive impact.

One case in my own organization involved a person who apparently saw an opportunity when a supervisor (not her supervisor) was eliminating a unit that was seriously losing money. She used this service in her work, but rather than try to make her case as to how this service supported her and examine the quite valid options that the supervisor had set up to meet her needs, she chose to attempt to destroy his credibility. She tried every trick in the book to discredit this supervisor. She badmouthed his performance, not only to me, but also to the whole department. She said the deficit in the unit that he was eliminating was his fault. She tried to find examples of him not treating his staff right. She, and this is the kicker, tried to get that unit assigned to her, which would have resulted in her making a higher salary.

There was more, but you get the idea. In fact, the last item was dominant. She was really trying to take over the units that the person she was attacking supervised. She had *lusted* over his job for a long time, so she used this opportunity to try to build her career at his expense. What she didn't know was that the supervisor and I had been trying to deal with this problem for a long time. In fact he had tried to defend this unit several times to me. But, "the handwriting was on the wall." The demand for this service had simply evaporated because technology had evolved to the point that people could do the job themselves. So finally, we together agreed that it was time to make a change (by the way, we created a soft landing for the person affected, who ended up with a better job). So the person who was trying to use political tactics made a bad choice as to who to attack. She didn't last long in our group!

I WOULD NOT TOLERATE OFFICE POLITICS

It may be clear to you from all of the other pronouncements I have made in previous chapters that I really do my absolute best to support my people. I make sure that no matter the circumstances, I try to take care of them, give them the benefit of the doubt, help them to improve, and solve their problems. Well, and I am putting this in all caps to emphasize the point: IN THE ORGANIZATIONS UNDER MY SUPERVISION, THE ONLY REASON THAT YOU CAN GET FIRED ON THE SPOT IS ENGAGING IN **OFFICE POLITICS**. Now, in reality in the bureaucracy I lived in, it was nearly impossible to fire someone on the spot, but trust me, anyone who committed this sin was the living dead and would be gone no matter how long it took me. Case in point, the person described above was "out of here" as soon as I had an excuse to do a lay off.

WHAT ARE THE IMPACTS OF OFFICE POLITICS

Why am I so "hard over" on this issue? There are a multitude of reasons.

Let's start with productivity. When people are subjected to an environment characterized by office politics they spend a substantial part of their time either: worrying about being attacked, defending themselves against those attacks, figuring out retaliatory attacks, or just planning and implementing strategies to advance at the expense of others. Just think about how much time these activities consume. How much time is wasted strategizing against the other guy, trying to defend your self against an attack, retaliating, or just worrying? It is an enormous amount of time that is not being spent doing the work of the organization. Even if you do not have an environment where people are trying to do their best, but just want to do enough to get by, office politics will distract them to the point where they are even less productive. It takes a lot of energy to fight these battles. After all you are, for all intents and purposes, fighting for your life – your home, food on the table for your kids, the new Lexus in your garage, whatever. The fight becomes more important than the work of your group! Just think how all of this reduces the productivity in your organization.

Now, how about motivation? As I said above, there are those who believe competition is good and will argue that this kind of competition leads to people trying harder to do their best. I assert that, in fact, it leads to people being less motivated to do their best. They perceive that no matter how hard they work or how much they are committed, the politics negate all of what they do. The politics are what matters. Productivity, quality, and hard work are subordinate because the political environment negates them. So why work hard, why try to do your best, why be committed to your organization? A sense of futility overcomes people. The work of the organization becomes secondary because it takes so much energy to play the political game and survive.

What about the quality of the product? My simple answer is how can the best product be produced when everyone is spending a large fraction of their time playing politics? The impact, however, goes even deeper. If their political opponents sabotage their work, then that product will not be as good as it could be.

Then, as I mentioned above, some people choose to hide out. They try to keep as low a profile as possible. Their strategy is to behave in such a way as to not represent a threat to people who are playing politics. How do you do this? First, you go precisely by the book. Of course, the book is often, or I should say more often than not, wrong. Also, you try to avoid doing anything to heighten your visibility, like doing an outstanding job or exhibiting creativity. Why? Because doing so could be perceived as upstaging the political person(s). Then that person(s) would launch an attack, which is just what you are trying to avoid. The result is the quality of the work of employees who are hiding out is low.

So what does this do to the work environment? It is pervaded by evil rather than support. It is cold and not nurturing. It is characterized by ruthlessness. It stimulates unethical behavior, rather than honesty. It makes trust almost impossible. It provides very little incentive for people to strive to be the best. In fact, in this environment people are not rewarded for excellence in their jobs, but excellence in fighting the political battles. In short, the work environment is as far to the opposite as you can get from the type of environment that we want to create.

OFFICE POLITICS DESTROYS HAPPINESS

Here is the downside that is critically important to me. Except for those few people who thrive on the fight, a culture characterized by office politics basically makes people unhappy in their jobs. Most of us just want to come to work, do our jobs the best we can, and go home. Instead you must engage in the constant battle to keep your job, you have feelings of uncertainty, insecurity, and fear. You are not able to trust anyone, so strong collegial relationships do not develop. You do not feel you are doing your best at your job – there is little sense of fulfillment.

Even worse is that all of these problems and feelings carry over into people's home life. As we talked about in previous chapters, it is almost impossible not to think about what is going on at work when you are at home. So generally all of these negative feelings pervade peoples' whole lives, not just their work lives. That is truly sad, because the happiness of the family is also degraded.

When people are subjected to a work environment like this, how committed, how loyal, how motivated do you think they will be? Will they really want to go the last mile for you? Will they look forward to coming to work? Will they get satisfaction from their jobs? Will you have an efficient productive organization? Will you be able to produce the best product? Of course, the answer to all these questions is an emphatic "No!". We can't get the best from our people if they are not happy!

THE WASHINGTON SYNDROME

Recall the Washington Syndrome I mentioned above. Although politics pervade many bureaucracies, for illustrative purposes here, I will give my (possibly a bit exaggerated and certainly cynical) view of government bureaucracies in Washington, D.C., because they represent the most visible and most seriously infected. The political environment that exists in the Senate, House of Representatives, and the Executive Branch represent a culture that is emulated in the bureaucracies. This is why nothing seems to ever really get done by the various agencies in Washington (just like in Congress). All you need to do is look at the performance of these organizations – slow, poor quality, indecisive, by the book (which doesn't fit most circumstances, but right or wrong, it is safe) – to see that they suffer from some cancerous disease. People are spending a large fraction of their time engaged in politics rather than doing the country's business. Just think about it. How much could get done for our country if the people in Washington focused on work, rather that paying attention to the internal politics of their organization? The government would cost a whole lot less, and we might be able to get a lot more done. Now it is gridlocked. Only a small portion of the real mission of the organization is addressed because everyone in the bureaucracy is positioning himself or herself to, in their minds, advance their careers or at least prevent them from being destroyed.

In fact, their careers probably will be advanced, because the tragedy is that at every level, managers and supervisors allow and even encourage this behavior. After all, it is the environment that they grew up in. Advancement is based more on how effectively you can beat down your peers, rather than how good a job you do. No one really thinks about what could be done if managers sought to create an environment where people strive to be the best at their jobs, rather than the best at politics. As I see it, even those people who do try to do their best lose in the end because they are consumed by the dog-eat-dog culture where winning the fight is more important than getting the job done.

While the leaders in bureaucracies, such as those that pervade our government, profess to have lofty goals for benefiting the taxpayers, their real, unspoken, and possibly even subconscious goal is to protect and build their bureaucracies. Just look at how it works: The bureaucracy is not getting the job done, but the solution is not to become more efficient and increase productivity, it is to argue for more resources. So it is not in the manager's best interest to have their people do their best because if they did, they might actually get the job done, and the managers would not be able to enlarge their organizations by adding more resources. Thus, they cannot justify being advanced in their careers and salaries. So, in my biased and cynical view, managers encourage political wrangling among their subordinates to minimize their efficiency so they can justify more resources.

HOW TO CURE THE DISEASE

How do we as managers prevent office politics from infecting our organization? The answer is really quite simple. You as the boss must make it unequivocally clear that this type of behavior is not acceptable, period. As I said before, my one rule was that the only way a person could get fired on the spot was to get caught engaging in office politics – attempting to build his career on the backs of fellow workers. You must really mean it. I did not hesitate to state this value publicly, and when it became necessary to implement the one rule, I made sure that people saw I really meant that it was fatal to engage in office politics. And, of course, you must "walk the talk" and try to avoid being political in your own behavior.

Office politics create an atmosphere where it is impossible to get the best from people. Every effort has to be made to eradicate office politics from your organization. The way to achieve this eradication is to make it highly visible to your staff that you will not tolerate behavior such as this under any circumstances, and set an example by your own behavior. In a family we all try to help each other and celebrate each other's success, we don't want anyone to fail, so we will rally around one of our own to help them when they are having difficulties. The last thing we want is for our siblings, brothers and sisters to be unhappy. This is the attitude that will insure that our work place is an environment where people give their best.

SECTION FOUR

THE BOTTOM LINE

What is all of this really about? We want to create the best possible workplace environment for our people, and the better it is the more they will strive to give their best in support of their family.

CHAPTER 4.1

WE ARE A FAMILY

The fundamental premise of this book is that employees will give their best if they perceive their workplace environment as a family.

Throughout this book the emphasis has been on how to stimulate employees to give their best. A list of values were presented that constitute a workplace environment wherein people give their best. Taken together these values define a workplace family.

I don't think this is a particularly new idea. How many times have you heard people who, along with their group, are being recognized for some accomplishment say something like "it was great, we worked together, and we were like a family"? I am not sure how often the leaders of such groups actually consciously set out to create a family spirit although I think this is rare. More often than not workplace families emerge serendipitously. Sometimes there is a charismatic leader who naturally brings people together in a way that creates a family atmosphere. Other times it is just natural fallout of the individuals in the group. They all *resonate* with each other in a special way. They did not set out to create a family, but may have had some special task or mission to which they were all committed. They worked together in a way that created synergism and a resultant success that gave them all a serious sense of mutual accomplishment and belonging.

A FAMILY IS NOT A TEAM

Although members of a team can feel like a family, a family is much more than a team. Teaming is often thought of as a motivational strategy. But, a team is a group of people who come together to undertake a discrete and specified task or project. While members of a team are diverse in their expertise, those different talents are complementary to one another in pursuit of a well-defined task. Each person's skills contribute to the body of knowledge that needs to be focused on a single task.

Attempts by managers to define a large diverse organization where the various components do not necessarily mutually contribute to the success of others as a team fail in the end. Often management in large organizations defines the whole organization as one big team – even calling their employees "Team Members." They are trying to generalize to a large group a strategy that works to motivate a small group, but what is missing is the sense of unity and mutual contribution to a given task. It is forced, like a square peg in a round hole. A family works where teams won't work. Why?

WHAT IS A FAMILY

A family is a collection of people who, rather than sharing a commitment to a specific task, share a special bond that goes beyond the specifics of their respective expertise or jobs. Members of a family are treated differently, better, than those outside. They are unified, loyal, and supportive of each other. They want the best for each other. Families stick together. There is a bond of love that holds them together. Even though they may sometimes fight, when it is over, they still love each other. They care about, watch out for, and defend each other. There is an innate trust. When one member of the family faces adversity, the others come together to help out. They celebrate each other's successes and see the success of one member as the success of them all.

It is these qualities that I have tried to instill in my organization. I will admit that it took some time. Naysayers and curmudgeons thought the idea was silly. They would argue: "This is a business, not a family, and it should be managed as such." My argument was simply that yes this is a business and as such our ultimate purpose is to make that business as successful as possible.

Creating a family feeling among the employees helps in a big way to achieve that success. Others would argue that many families are pathological and have just the opposite characteristics that I so idealistically described. My answer to this is that there are sick families, but the combination of the positive values I recommend plus a management commitment to attack any of those maladies when they arise will insure success. Eventually, however, everyone did buy off on the concept.

A healthy family environment has a number of characteristics that are consistently found: honesty, acceptance of individuals for themselves, recognizing our humanness, being humane, recognizing that work and life are one, having pride, in fact all of the values I have described are characteristics that can be found in a family. In each chapter I mention how the value discussed therein related to a family environment.

In the cases of workplace families that emerge spontaneously there is a bit of a "chicken or egg" issue. How many of the family friendly values I have described stimulated the development of the family or were a result of it? That is a good question, and I have no answer. But, the question is moot herein because I argue that by following my approach the values are incorporated into the workplace first and the family idea is consistently mentioned a workplace family will emerge.

In my own case at the Scripps Institution of Oceanography I came to believe that by heightening the visibility of the family idea and immersing people in a positive value based environment I could achieve even greater success with my group. From all that I had read and seen I was sure it would improve my chances of achieving my ultimate goal, so I set out to create a family atmosphere, and I did, and it had exactly the effect I had hoped for -- it worked.

HOW DO YOU CREATE A FAMILY

How do you create this family spirit? It really isn't that hard. As I mentioned before, the values I use in my approach to managing people are reflective of, and stimulate, a family atmosphere. Given the existence of this value system, the next most import component is that you must honestly and sincerely adopt and radiate the family spirit yourself. Then, it simply amounts to a sustained PR campaign. Basically you talk it up, apply the concept wherever and whenever you can. For example, I would always refer to our group as "our family." Our unit heads meeting was "Family Council." Whenever someone did something nice for another person, it was the "family thing to do." Similarly, when choices had to be made about people or situations in the group, I would ask, "What is the family way to do this?" The point is that you simply run the commercial over and over. Then, as real family-like feelings start to develop between people, you amplify, reinforce, and encourage others to see them and behave in that way toward each other.

IT REALLY WORKS

I consider my success in creating this "family" as one of the most important accomplishments of my entire career. It was great because I felt it too. It was a wonderful feeling for me, as well as the others in the rest of our little family. I know that I felt, and I believe the others felt, a desire to do our best so the whole group would look good. Sometimes there would be disagreements between persons in the family, but they were mostly resolved quickly, and long-term grudges were never held. But, let someone from the outside try to do something to one of our own, and the whole group would rally to his defense. We did not have destructive competition between one another. Instead we celebrated each other's successes and took them on as our own. More than that, most people sincerely developed a commitment to our family that will probably never leave them. There was a spirit, a feeling, and a sense that we were all part of something more than just a workplace. Loyalty developed that was beyond just the loyalty that people sometimes feel for a company. There was a trust of one another that I rarely saw among staff in other organizations.

I said early on that one of the principle objectives of my method of motivating people to do their best was to give them a sense of belonging. I tried to create an environment where people wanted to come to work. This environment should be welcoming and supportive, where people felt good about what they were doing, good about the people around them, and good about the place they work. The sense of family is one of the most important aspects of successfully accomplishing those goals.

The family spirit is one of the most important values among those that establish a positive workplace climate that stimulates people to do their best. Families are not teams, but teams can be families. A family unifies people in a special way that gives them a feeling of belonging and mutual support that no other organizational or motivational strategy can. Actually, creating a family spirit in your organization is easier than you may think. Just believe in it yourself, and then talk it up.

CHAPTER 4.2

LOVE

If your heart is in it, everyone wins.

I have been advised not to include this chapter or at least give it a different title. Some people seem to think it may appear too gushy or will be misinterpreted. But, I can't leave it out because I think the idea herein is the overarching value that permeates all of the other values described in previous chapters. It represents one of the key criteria for selecting these values and for rejecting others. It is possibly the most important component of successfully achieving our goal – to create a healthy workplace family. After all, what is it that truly binds members of a family together? And, the fundamental premise of this book is that people will give their best if they are immersed in a workplace with a strong family spirit.

BE A LEADER

In the multitude of texts on leadership you will consistently find that a key characteristic of a real leader is that you "walk the talk." That is basically true, but you will also find that a key personality trait needed to be an effective leader is: *"You must have a sincere, enthusiastic, and passionate commitment to creating the best possible work environment for your people – one where you have a personal stake in their success, and they know it."*

YOU HAVE A VESTED INTEREST

Up front, from a pedestrian standpoint, we do in fact have a stake in the success of our people. As I pointed out in the beginning of this book, the more successful our people are, the more successful we as managers will be. When they do their best, the productivity of your unit is best, and the best quality product is produced. But, is that enough?

The personal stake I am talking about here goes beyond the outward trappings of success. If you are just a practical, by the book, manager and you go about implementing all of the recommendations in this book without internalizing the values (walking the talk) implicit therein on an emotional level, it is likely that you may not achieve the goal of getting the best from your people. If you have a sincere, enthusiastic, and passionate commitment to creating the best possible work environment for your people, it says that you have a stake in their well-being and their happiness. If you are focused on those goals, then you will get their best.

In the simplest words possible: "It won't work if your heart isn't in it."

YOU MUST REALLY CARE

What do I mean by this? Let me try to explain. Leaders are not leaders unless, at the most fundamental level, they care about their followers. At the deepest level they define their vision as making "it" better for their people, whatever "it" is. Gandhi, Patton, and other great leaders all deeply cared about the welfare of those who followed them, which, in turn, endowed their followers with loyalty, devotion, and commitment.

While I hate to admit it, even megalomaniacs like James Jones and David Karesh were able to lead their people to their ultimate end because the people believed that their leaders really cared for them and loved them, and in their own twisted way, they probably did. While most of us have a hard time believing this, it is true and has been demonstrated many times. When a leader loves, or can convincingly show that he loves his followers, the followers will trust him, believe essentially anything he preaches, and essentially do anything that he wants them to do: turn over all their assets, shun society in general, grow their own food, and even commit mass suicide or, on a positive note, give their all to support his goals.

I am not talking about romantic love or sexual love, but instead the kind of love expressed in the biblical statement that: "God so loved us that he gave his only begotten son for us." Don't worry; I am not talking about religion here either. What I am talking about is that the leader really, really cares about the people below him. He loves them.

When I say that the leader has a personal stake in his people's success, I am going beyond the stake that makes him successful such as efficiency, productivity, and quality products. What I am talking about is a real and honest desire to see his followers successful *for its own sake*. It is the sense that the leader derives real meaning in his own life from helping his people to be successful, to create a situation where they have meaning in their lives, and to do as much as possible to make it possible for them to be happy in their jobs. Wanting to create an environment like this for his people is an expression of love for them. But, it is also an indirect approach to achieving more pedestrian goals. If your highest priority is to give people the best work life possible, then the other trappings of success will come automatically.

THE POWER OF LOVE

Walt Disney was one of the most inspired leaders that I have been able to find. To this day, many years after his death, his spirit and the tone he set for his organization are still pervasive and inspire one of the most successful organizations in the world. Why? As I learned when I was fortunate enough to participate in a "Disney Approach to People Management" seminar, the mission set down by Walt Disney for both the guests and cast at his theme parks was: "To Create Happiness." Wow, could you get behind that mission? I sure can, and I see that mission as an expression of love. I suggest it for those of you who are reading this book and want to achieve the goals I set out.

This is the power of love, and I argue that if your leadership is an expression of love, then you cannot fail. Here I mean that if you focus on adopting the values I have outlined in this book for the sake of giving people a better life, then the pedestrian rewards will come to you in greater volume than you could ever imagine. If your love for your people is real and you really care about creating a great life for them, they will give you more than their all. You will get their best and beyond. Your organization will be a success. Your career will advance, you will make more money, and most of all, you will have an innate sense that what you are doing is, in the most fundamental way, good. It is a morally right thing to do, which standing by itself is a profound accomplishment that will bring you a deep inner satisfaction and an enduring sense that your life has meant something more than just making money or producing widgets.

FIELD THEORY

For those of you who have some knowledge of physics, or even for those of you who don't, you probably know of the concept of a "field." There are, for example, magnetic fields, gravitational fields, etc. A field is a property of an object that enables it to have an effect on objects at a distance from it. A piece of iron placed near a magnet will be attracted to the magnet. The magnet creates a magnetic field that affects the iron. If you put iron filings near a magnet the particles will align themselves along the "magnetic field lines." Similarly, the earth creates a gravitational field, which attracts things to it. That is why we all don't go floating out into space.

Likewise, I have come to believe that feelings held by one person create a field that affects people around him. You have all felt it. You come into a room where something difficult or emotional is being discussed and you "feel the tension in the room." You go to a party where everyone is having a great time. You feel the energy and start having a great time too. The examples are endless. My point is that if you are able to feel the kind of love I am describing here for your people, it will create a field that will affect them. Feelings are infectious because the field you create radiates them. The field created by your feelings will give the people around you good feelings, and even better, the field will affect them so that they will begin to have similar feelings for their colleagues and peers. And, each of them will radiate a field that influences others in a positive way. They will begin to love each other. It is at that point where you have created a real workplace family -- the sense of support, caring, loyalty, commitment, and all of the other positive characteristics of people who do their best will permeate the whole organization.

LET YOURSELF FEEL IT

Some of you might reject this idea out of hand saying: "That's all a bunch of hippy, touchy-feely claptrap." I will say it again. If that is how you think, you will not achieve a level of success that is beyond normal expectations. The real bottom line is that you have to put aside your prejudice and let yourself feel love for your people. To repeat: *let yourself.* I emphasize this point because often people's inhibitions prevent them from exhibiting such emotions. "It is not manly to exhibit such emotions." "People might get the wrong idea." "Feelings just get in the way." None of this is true but if they represent the way you feel, a field will radiate that spreads those emotions. Let yourself feel love for your people. It really isn't that hard, and the field you create will instill positive feelings throughout your organization.

HOW TO DO IT

Once you have accepted and allowed yourself to feel it, in a real way, how do you express love as I have defined it and permeate the environment that we want to create with it? Just read the chapters. Every value that I have put forth can, and should, be expressed with love. Let me mention a few: we reject office politics because, among other things, they make people feel badly; we want people to fit in because if they don't they will feel like outcasts; we want to treat people humanely because to treat them otherwise would make them unhappy; we want to establish a spirit of family because families have love. Just think about the rest of them. You will see that in essence they are all expressions of love.

Ask yourself how you can implement these values with love. They are about caring, giving people meaning in their lives, being the inspiration for them to treat all the people around them with the same spirit, they are about setting a tone that is supportive, secure, meaningful, inspiring, and happy. Your mission as a leader should be to *create happiness* among your employees. The field you create will permeate your workplace and then you win – for your organization, for your people, and for yourself.

Section Five

It Works

Finally – "How do I make it happen?"

CHAPTER 5.1

IMPLEMENTATION

Can you make this program work in your organization?

Achieving the goals I have defined requires implementation of a program involving integration of a set of positive values into the culture of your organization. These specific values are described in the chapters that comprise the bulk of this book. They provide a foundation upon which a healthy workplace family can be built. Here I will outline for you the steps that can be taken to successfully implement the program.

CULTURAL CHANGE MUST OCCUR – MANAGE IT CORRECTLY

In going forward, you need to keep in mind that what you are doing is implementing a fundamental change in the culture of your organization. Change, especially in an organization's culture, is very difficult in any organization. I advocate the evolutionary approach where changes occur over an extended period of time. It is a process wherein after a period of time people stop and say: "Hey . . . ah, we used to (blank) but now we are (blank). How did that happen?" In this way, the negative emotions – fear, uncertainty, misunderstandings, etc. – attendant to change are minimized.

Sudden change is the least effective. So, if you call a staff meeting, stand before the group and say: "People, as of today we will be living according to the following set of values, and we will be a happy family…" you are likely to be laughed out of the room. And, it will never work.

Evolutionary change takes time, so does cultural change. Don't be impatient – take your time. None of this will happen over night.

PROGRAM MUST BE COMPREHENSIVE

Here is one other extremely important matter. Your program must be comprehensive. By that I mean that all of the values I list in this book must be implemented. These particular values were selected after trial and error from a broad universe of possible values that could be applied. They fit together and, in most cases, are overlapping and mutually supportive of each other. No matter which value you pick, it can be related to at least one and often several of the others.

This is not to say that they are redundant. Each has its own basic content. But, the overlap reinforces and strengthens their effectiveness. It is for this reason it is essential that the whole program be implemented to create a comprehensive positive value-based workplace environment. I cannot emphasize enough that a total environment must be created that is governed by the set of values provided here.

Picking and choosing one or the other will not get the job done because of their interrelatedness. It is like bricks in a wall. If one or more are left out, the wall will be weak and eventually fail. If one or more values are missing, then the others that they reinforce will loose a part of their strength. In turn, as those are weakened they negatively affect the others that they interact with. Thus, the whole program is weakened to the point where very little will be accomplished.

GET A "NEW ATTITUDE"

As you go through these steps I hope you will do so with the recognition that the process really represents adopting an *attitude* toward managing people that is probably much different from other approaches you have heard of or studied. It involves you as a manager at the personal, emotional, and psychological levels. While, as I have discussed previously, the bottom line hoped for outcome is the classical trappings of success – money, status, etc. – approaching this program with an attitude that focuses on those measures will likely lead to failure. Your attitude must reflect confidence that they will be a secondary outcome of focusing on the direct personal benefits for your people, your organization, and yourself.

You, the manager, are the most important factor in successfully implementing this program. You must make a deeply felt personal commitment to creating a workplace environment – a family -- that gives your people a better overall life experience. This is the definition of successful implementation of this program – creating a better life for you people. Personally, you must seek the intrinsic rewards of achieving this outcome for others. This is not an easy process, and for some it will be impossible. It will require you to do some serious soul searching, evaluation of what, in the end, life is all about, and assimilation of the values into your own life space. Living by this value system will make it much easier to internalize this commitment, and once you have, you will be ready to go on with the implementation.

WALK THE TALK

Recall that a fundamental of leadership is "walking the talk." If at this point you have assimilated the values you are trying to incorporate into you organizational culture, you have taken the first step. Now, you must demonstrate behaviors consistent with the value system. People will see this intuitively. The "Field Theory" that I described in the previous chapter in essence says the spirit (or vibes) that a person radiates influences the feelings of people around him. By just incorporating these values into your persona, you will influence the people around you through radiation of your field. They will become infected and spontaneously begin to behave in accordance with the values.

Still, radiating vibes is not enough. As people begin to intuitively perceive you behaving in a certain way, you must take every opportunity to reinforce specific values by mentioning them in the context of your actions. This opportunistic approach provides a subtle way of bringing values to the forefront.

Make sure that your decisions, actions, and pronouncements be visibly based on the values you want to be assimilated into your organization's culture. Mention the value or values behind these behaviors. For example, if some one makes an error, deal with it as a learning experience and say that you value treating errors as such.

Talk it up on every occasion that you can. Remember, the key is to create a workplace family. Every time you have a chance refer to the group as a family – remember "Family Council"? Keep saying it, and eventually people will see the group as a family and see themselves as part of that family.

Make sure to openly and visibly reward people for behaviors that are consistent with important values. Thank people publicly for helping each other, being honest, celebrating each other's successes, etc.

Make sure that you openly and visibly act on occasions when values are violated. An example is "office politics." A key value is rejection of this type of behavior. When it occurs, make sure that it is clear to people that you will not stand for it.

So, in the end, successful implementation of this program is simply creating a better life for your people. Fundamentally, there are two steps. First, assimilate the values yourself and make the commitment to give people a better life. Secondly, just go on a PR campaign. Think of Budweiser or Coke. They do run in-your-face ads, but the preponderance of their marketing involves having their name everywhere you look. This is subtle, but it works. And, what I am saying is that this subtle approach as outlined above will lead to success.

Again, the thesis behind this program is that creating a work life family for your employees will cause them to give their best. The list of positive values I have presented here has proven to work when comprehensively implemented. But, there may be others that will help too. Do not be afraid to try additional values; there are more than likely others out there that can augment my program. But, please do not do so by eliminating one or more of the values I have defined.

CHAPTER 5.2

THAT'S ALL FOLKS

In the preface to this book I said that writing it was a compulsion. The fact is that I felt I had created a way of managing people that resulted in their having a better life than they otherwise would. The practical result of this management approach is that people will give their best to you and your organization.

Remember, when I began pulling these concepts together for several talks I was invited to give, I entitled it "Lucky." I am lucky, not just because of all of the normal trappings of success (e.g. great house, wife, kids, etc.), but because as a manager of people, I was in a position to create this program. To me, giving my people a better life is an accomplishment that supersedes all others and has given me a sense that I have contributed something good -- it made my life better too.

Now I feel even luckier because I have been able write this book with the hope that it will give other managers the opportunity I had to make their people's lives, and their own life, better. This is why I felt compelled to write the book. My hope is that it is written well enough and that I have been clear and convincing enough that you, the reader, will go ahead and try it.

If, in fact, you have gotten this far, chances are that you did find this approach interesting and possibly worth a try. If so, then I thank you and wish you the best of luck. Remember, it will take time, but be persistent and don't give up. But, in the end, it is up to you, and trust me it is really worth it.

Tom Collins
September 2010

Since his graduation from UCLA with BS/Engineering and MBA degrees, Tom Collins has spent his entire career in positions involving the management of people. He has published papers on management topics and spoken widely at professional conferences and in many other forums on topics of administration, information systems, people management, and the Scripps Institution of Oceanography where he spent the last 21 years as the chief administrative officer. He now serves as Emeritus Deputy Director and Associate Vice Chancellor at the Scripps Institution of Oceanography, University of California, San Diego. He resides in Pine Valley California with his wife, Karen and four dogs.